Winning
GOLF FOR
WOMEN

Winning
GOLF FOR
WOMEN

BEVERLY LEWIS

CollinsWillow

An Imprint of HarperCollinsPublishers

First published in 1993 by
Collins Willow
an imprint of HarperCollins*Publishers*
London

A CIP catalogue record for this book
is available from the British Library

ISBN 0 00 218521 0

Designed and produced by
MasterClass Design Ltd
37 Seymour Close, Birmingham B29 7JD

Photography by Ken Lewis and Visions in Golf
Illustrations by Ken Lewis

Colour origination by Colourscan, Singapore
Printed and bound in Italy by
OFSA S.p.A.

Contents

INTRODUCTION

Whether you are a beginner or a more experienced club golfer this book will help you to improve your golf, enabling you to enjoy your game even more.

No beginner at golf can become immediately proficient. It is only by learning and practising that any of us can improve. That rate of improvement does, however, vary from person to person, depending on one's natural ability and on how much time is available to practise or play.

I can assure you that even the best women golfers in the world have to practise in order to keep their game sharp and to keep their particular swing faults under control. Make no mistake, every golfer has faults and depending on how severe those faults may be and how much the player works to keep them in check, it will affect their scores.

You will find that there are certain swing preferences that I believe are important and that I teach my pupils. Ideally I would like all my pupils to swing incorporating every one of these principles, but we are not machines and we all swing differently according to our size and strength. To help illustrate this point, I have included photographs of several top players and you will see that, for one reason or another, not all are entirely orthodox, but use a method that works for them. I hope you will learn to understand the golf swing and how to recognise and correct your particular faults.

Because golf demands such a high degree of accuracy, it is best learnt in stages. Initially most beginners find that nothing they are asked to do involving either the grip or the address position feels natural and, because of this, they feel it is incorrect.

Conversely, what feels more comfortable is usually considered by the player to be correct, when more often than not the opposite is true. For the more experienced golfer who has played for some time with a fault, altering the swing can be much more difficult. In this book you will find the answers to most problems, but remember, there is no gain without pain!

Whilst some of my pupils do not practise too much between lessons, preferring just to play, those who do practise certainly improve more quickly. This does not necessarily mean that

Without some practice you will never achieve your full potential as a golfer.

you have to spend endless hours on a practice ground as even a few minutes a day swinging a club in your garden will help you to make improvements in your swing. Putting indoors on a carpet can improve even the most erratic putting action. That will definitely lower your scores.

One of the great joys of golf is that you do not have to be particularly fit to play it. Of course, someone who is fit will not tire during a round like an unathletic beginner, but the more you play the fitter you will become. Remember that physical fitness promotes mental fitness and you will not find your ability waning towards the end of the round.

I have included some exercises which will help you to strengthen your golfing muscles. Certainly strength is an asset, though not a necessity, but since most women are not as physically strong as men, I believe that our technique has to be better in order to make up for this disparity.

There is one department of golf that does not really need strength, and that is the short game. However, it is a very much neglected aspect, and one that too few players practise. Don't make that mistake; apply as much time to the short game as you do to the full swing and I will guarantee that your scores will tumble quite dramatically.

So what is needed to make a good golfer? First of all I would say that determination is very important, and the golfer who will keep trying and persevering until she succeeds may well turn out a better player than someone with more natural ability but less drive. Golf is a difficult game and so often we do not get the rewards we think we deserve, so patience is required along with the self-discipline to practise, or just to keep one's temper when something goes wrong on the course.

But most of all the successful golfer is one who enjoys the game. This may be someone who never gets her handicap below, say, 20, but who derives great pleasure from being in such delightful surroundings as a golf course, hitting

Lessons from a golf professional are vital, particularly when you begin golf, in order to avoid mistakes which could take a long time to put right.

the occasional good shot and enjoying the social side of the game.

I hope that this book will make you a more successful golfer and someone who gets the most from their ability, whatever that may be. Golf is your hobby, so make the most of every round, and if you have had fun, then you're a winner.

Finally, my sincere thanks to PING golf clubs for their superb equipment, to Titleist for the gloves and golf balls and to Stylo for making walking the fairways so comfortable.

For the location photographs my thanks to Mr Kawaguchi and professional Juan Parron at Almerimar Golf Club, Spain.

Lastly, my great thanks for the photographs and illustrations, for his patience and knowledge, to my husband Ken Lewis, without whose help and encouragement this book would not have been written.

TERMINOLOGY

To help you to follow the text clearly, it will be useful for you to know some of the more widely used golfing terms and what they mean, so the following should serve as a reference where necessary.

Address: The position taken opposite the ball prior to hitting it.

Angle of attack: The angle of descent of the clubhead towards the ball.

Arc: The curved path of the clubhead during the swing.

Backspin: The spin that is imparted to the ball when it is struck correctly, and which causes the ball to rise.

Backswing: The movement of the clubhead away from the ball, until it begins its downward journey.

Closed:

(a) The clubface is aimed to the left of the target line at address or impact.

(b) The clubface aims towards the sky at the top of the backswing.

(c) At address, when the body aims too much to the right.

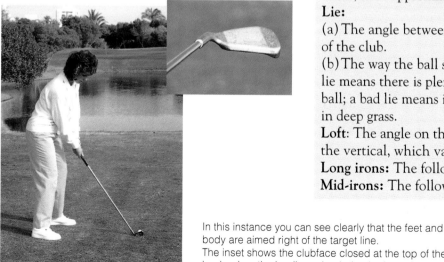

Divot: A small piece of turf removed from the ground by the clubhead, or the hole left in the ground by this action.

Down the line: The view of the swing taken standing to the right of the player looking towards the target.

Downswing: The movement of the clubhead back towards the ball from the top of the backswing.

Draw: A controlled right-to-left movement of the ball in the air.

Fade: A controlled left-to-right movement of the ball in the air.

Grip: The position adopted by the hands on the club, and also the rubber tubing that is fitted to the top of the club shaft.

Hook: A sharp right-to-left movement of the ball in the air.

In-to-in: The swing path of the clubhead through impact when it travels from inside the target line, and travels back to the inside after impact. In clock face terms, 3.30–9.00–8.30.

In-to-out: The swing path of the clubhead through impact when it travels from inside the target line to the outside of it. In clock face terms, from approximately 4 to 10 o'clock.

Lie:

(a) The angle between the sole and the shaft of the club.

(b) The way the ball sits on the grass; a good lie means there is plenty of grass beneath the ball; a bad lie means it may sit in a divot or be in deep grass.

Loft: The angle on the clubface measured from the vertical, which varies from club to club.

Long irons: The following irons: 1, 2, 3, 4.

Mid-irons: The following irons: 5, 6, 7.

In this instance you can see clearly that the feet and body are aimed right of the target line.
The inset shows the clubface closed at the top of the backswing, the leading edge being horizontal.

My feet and body are aiming left of the target here and (inset) the clubface is open at the top of the backswing, the leading edge being almost vertical.

Open:

(a) The clubface looks to the right of the target line at address or impact.

(b) The toe of the club points downwards too much at the top of the backswing.

(c) At address when the body aims too much to the left.

Out-to-in: The swing path of the clubhead through impact when it travels from the outside of the target line to the inside of it. In clock face terms, from approximately 2 to 8 o'clock.

Posture: The angle of the spine, head, and flex of the legs at address, when viewed down the line.

Pull: A shot that travels straight left.

Push: A shot that travels straight right.

Set-up: The same as the address.

Shallow attack: When the clubhead is approaching the ball travelling fairly parallel to the ground.

Short irons: The following irons: 8, 9, wedge and sand-wedge.

Slice: A severe left-to-right movement of the ball in the air.

Square:

(a) The clubface sits at right angles to the target line at address or at impact.

(b) The correct position at the top of the backswing, where the clubface is approximately 45° to the horizontal.

(c) At address when the body is parallel to the target line.

Stance: The position of the feet at address.

Steep attack: When the clubhead approaches the ball from a fairly vertical angle.

Strong grip: When either or both hands are placed too much to the right on the grip.

Swing path: The circular path of the clubhead during the swing.

Swing plane: The angle of the swing path, best viewed down the line.

Target line: An imaginary line drawn from the ball to the target.

Weak grip: When either or both hands are placed too much to the left on the grip.

Wrist cock: The upward hinging of the wrists on the backswing and through swing.

With correct alignment my feet and shoulders are square to the target and (inset) the clubface is at about 45°.

GETTING STARTED

It is, I think, very important when you learn to play golf, that you have a clear understanding of what it is you are trying to achieve. This does not mean that you have to become very technical, but it will help you to learn or to improve your game if you can see logically the reasons for doing certain things.

Because the golf clubface is rather small compared, say, to a tennis racquet, and the golf ball itself looks like a marble compared to a tennis ball, tolerance of inaccuracies in golf is very limited. If you contact the ball with the club half an inch out of position you will not have hit the ball correctly.

However, taking into consideration that you will have swung the club about 20 feet in a circular motion before impact, to be half an inch out is really quite good, but sadly in golf not quite good enough to produce your best shots. Please don't let these words deter you because, initially, you must learn to address the ball and to make a simple half swing trying to incorporate the correct actions.

Eventually these will result in your being able to hit the ball quite acceptably. Good contact follows as you play and practise more, so patience is the watchword.

PICTURING THE SWING

I want to give you a clear picture of what we are trying to make the clubhead do in the swing because, although you may be concentrating on moving particular parts of the body in certain ways, the ball only reacts to the clubhead.

As you stand to the ball, imagine that it is in the middle of a clock face on the ground, that you are standing at 6 o'clock and the target is at 9 o'clock. Initially the clubhead will swing back towards 3 o'clock for a short distance, then as the body turns and the arms swing upwards the club will travel towards 3.30 and then up to the top of the backswing.

Ideally, on the downswing the clubhead will virtually retrace its backswing path and approach the ball from the 3.30 direction, strike the ball as it moves towards the target at 9 o'clock and then travel inwards towards 8.30 as the body turns through to face the target. To hit the ball straight towards the target the clubface must be square to the target at impact. The path that the clubhead travels on is called the swing path.

The best swing path will take the clubhead through impact from about 3.30 to 8.30.

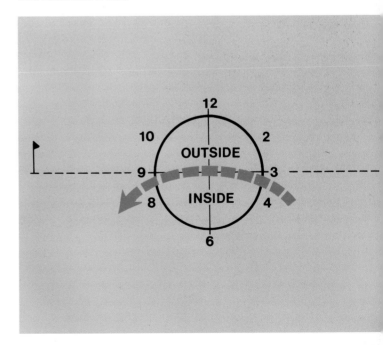

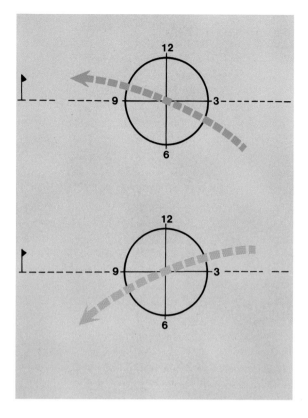

An in-to-out swing (above) and an out-to-in swing path. Both are technically incorrect for a shot hit straight.

Thus, when the club travels in the correct direction, it is described as travelling from 'in to straight to in', which is generally referred to as 'in-to-in'.

If the clubhead travels too much from the inside, i.e. more from 4 o'clock to 10 o'clock, this is called 'in-to-out'; and if the clubhead travels more from 2 o'clock to 8 o'clock, this is called 'out-to-in'.

You can see that the clubhead can travel in one of three main directions, with different degrees of out-to-in and in-to-out, which affects the ball's flight.

The other factor which has a major bearing on where the ball flies is the position of the clubface at impact. I have already mentioned that it must be square to the target for the ball to fly straight. If it is aimed to the right of the target at impact, called 'open', the ball will go to the right; and if it is aimed to the left of the target, called 'closed', the ball will go to the left.

It is quite possible to have a combination of any three swing paths and any three clubface positions at impact and this is what leads to erratic shots. My aim is to teach you to hit straight shots.

An imaginary line drawn back from the target, passing through 9 o'clock, the ball and 3 o'clock is called the target line. The area between this line and you is called 'inside' and the area beyond the line is called 'outside'.

The effect on the ball of various clubface positions. In (A) the clubface is open leading to a slice; (B) is square with a straight shot and (C) is closed, which causes a hook.

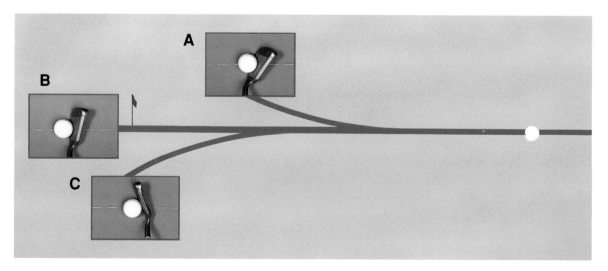

EQUIPMENT YOU WILL NEED

Until such time as you know that you are hooked on this game, it is not necessary to buy a complete set of golf clubs. However, even as a total beginner there are do's and don'ts in equipment. Initially, just one club, perhaps a 6- or 7-iron is sufficient to learn how to swing.

Try to buy or borrow one that has a good grip which is not too shiny and worn, but dull and not slippery. I would recommend that you use ladies' clubs, which feel lighter when swung, are more flexible in the shaft, and have thinner grips than men's clubs. If you are a stronger, more athletic person with medium to large size hands then you could use a man's club, providing it does not feel too heavy for you.

Good golfers control the club, and for the beginner this is a problem. Heavy clubs make the task more difficult, so avoid them. Once you have advanced a little and wish to play on a course, then you can look towards buying a set or half set of clubs.

Nowadays there is such a variety of clubs available and at the end of this book is some more detailed advice about what clubs should suit you. Whenever you buy equipment, consult a P.G.A. (Professional Golfers' Association) professional for sound advice.

Regarding footwear and clothing, much will depend on where you play, and the standard that is demanded.

If you are learning at a driving range, then rubber soled golf shoes or trainers are best, as each of these will give you a better grip on the mats. Be warned though, many clubs will not allow you to wear trainers on the golf course.

Metal studded golf shoes certainly give the best and most reliable grip when playing on grass. It is not essential that you wear a golf glove (worn on the left hand for right-handed players) to give better contact with the club,

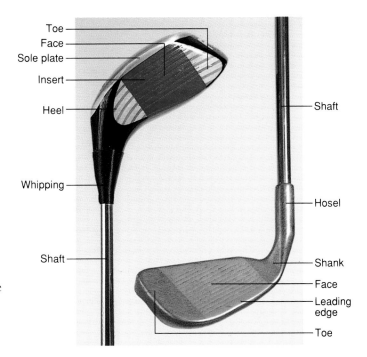

The different parts of a golf club, both a wood (left) and an iron (right).

but since most of the best players in the world wear one, then it must be worth considering. Buy one that fits snugly, as they tend to stretch. Old loose-fitting car driving gloves are useless, so treat yourself perhaps to an all-weather glove, which will be longer lasting than a more expensive leather one.

Fortunately, many of today's manufacturers present us with an attractive array of golfing clothes, but remember that the golf course is not the place to wear skimpy clothing in order to attain a superb suntan.

Generally most clubs will allow Bermuda length shorts and sleeveless shirts in summer, but sun tops are definitely taboo. In colder weather, wear several layers of thin clothing, rather than chunky knitwear. You will find that thermal underwear will keep you very warm.

Most golf clubs and the majority of golfers uphold the high standard of etiquette that has made the game so envied by other sports, so please do your best to observe the dress code required by the club at which you play.

THE GRIP

Golfers are lucky in that, prior to hitting the ball, they have an unlimited (though do not take that too literally!) amount of time in which to prepare themselves.

For instance, you may have the best tennis backhand in the world but if you are not in the right position on the court to hit the ball as it comes to you, then that ability is irrelevant.

Please do not underestimate the importance of a good address position in golf. If the static part of the game is wrong, then the swing will undoubtedly be adversely affected. The beauty of attaining a good set-up is that it can be, and indeed in my opinion is, best practised indoors in front of a mirror, where you can see exactly what you are doing.

One simple fact to remember in golf is that what we are doing and what we *feel* we are doing are very often two entirely different things. So let's look at what a good address position consists of, and if you can practise what follows in this chapter where you can see yourself, then so much the better.

so do take time to acquire what I believe is one of the most important fundamentals of golf.

With the clubface square to the target, position the grip so that it sits under the pad at the heel of the hand and lays diagonally across the palm resting in the forefinger. The end of the grip should not dig into your palm, so allow about a quarter of an inch to extend beyond

With the left hand first let the grip of the club lay across the palm from the heel of the hand to the first joint of the index finger.

THE LEFT HAND

Your hands are your sole contact with the club, and their job is to control the clubface, and to return it squarely back to the ball at impact. Most beginners find the correct grip feels far from natural and tend to grip the club in a manner that feels comfortable, but which is, in fact, incorrect.

A good grip does not guarantee that you will be a good golfer, but a poor grip means that you will have to make compensations in your swing and you will never get the best out of yourself,

The fingers then close around the club but be certain to leave about a quarter of an inch of the grip extending.

your palm. This will mean your little finger will be about an inch from the end of the grip.

Now close the fingers around the grip, and position the thumb just to the right of centre. Do not stretch your thumb down the shaft as this will cause tension in the muscles at the front of the forearm. The last three fingers, rather than the thumb and forefinger, should provide most of the pressure. This will place the club in the palm and the fingers of the left hand, providing a very secure and snug fit.

Hold the club up in front of you and you will see that two to two-and-a-half knuckles are visible, and that the 'V' formed by your thumb and forefinger points to the right side of your face, approximately to your eye.

To test if your grip is correct hold the club out horizontally in front of you, and release the thumb and last three fingers. If your grip is correct the club will now balance under the heel of your hand and in the crook of your forefinger. If you have placed the club too much in the centre of your palm rather than diagonally across it, the club will probably fall to the ground.

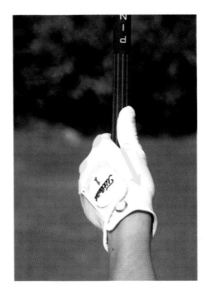

Far left: The correct left hand grip has the thumb comfortably positioned on the shaft just right of centre as you look down.

Left: By holding the club up in the air you should be able to see two to two-and-a-half knuckles on your left hand.

Below: If you grip the club correctly you should be able to extend your arm with the club held by the heel of the hand and the crook of your forefinger. The club should then balance without falling to the ground.

THE RIGHT HAND

Whilst the left hand is a palm and finger grip, the right hand is solely a finger grip, and to help you to appreciate how your right hand should feel I want you to take a golf ball in your right hand as if you were about to throw it a long way overarm.

Now look at how you are holding the ball and you will see that you are holding it mainly in your fingers and not very tightly. This will encourage your wrist to flex backwards as your arm moves forwards, giving you that snap in the wrist just as you release the ball. Remember, you are not holding the ball tightly, but in a technically correct manner, and that is how you should grip the club.

Now move the ball more into your palm and make the same movement; you will find that much of the flexibility in your wrist has gone.

Although you will have a firmer grip on the ball your ability to throw it a long way has diminished, and this is similar to how many players place their right hand on the grip. It feels more powerful, but in fact is weaker.

To attain the correct right hand grip place it so that the palm faces the target, with the grip at the base of the fingers.

Close your fingers around the grip, feeling that the right forefinger is slightly triggered and therefore very slightly separated from the middle two. The little finger should rest either on top of the left forefinger (if you have small hands) or between it and the left middle finger. The thumb should sit just to the left of centre on the grip.

The left thumb will sit snugly in the palm of the right hand, and is invisible when viewed face on. The right forefinger sits very much at the side of, rather than under, the grip. The 'V' of the right hand is virtually parallel to that of the left and therefore points just inside the right shoulder. Again, the best way to monitor your grip is to hold the club up in front of you.

Check the position of both 'V's; the number of knuckles visible on the left hand should be two to two-and-a-half.

As you progress at this game, so your grip may

By holding a ball in your fingers (left) you have a greater wrist flexibility than if you hold it more in the palm of your hand (right).

need to alter slightly according to how much hand action you are capable of producing, but the guidelines I have given should be acceptable for most players.

If, after reading this, you realise that your grip is far from perfect, persevere with the change. Initially it may feel terrible and the results may not instantly inspire you, but remember that a sound grip is the basis of a sound swing.

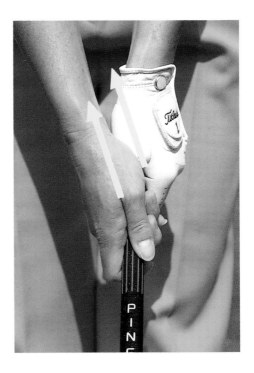

Then close the fingers around the grip, leaving the index finger slightly triggered. Again, the view from the front (above) and from the side (below).

To introduce the right hand to the grip, place it so that the palm is facing the target. The view from the front (above) and from the side (below).

GRIP PRESSURE

The club is gripped mainly by the last three fingers of the left hand and the middle two of the right, but be careful of your interpretation of the word grip. If there was a scale of 1 to 10, with 1 being very light and 10 being very tight, the correct pressure would be about 6 to 7.

More players grip the club too tightly than too lightly, mainly in the fear that the club will go flying out of their hands if they do not do so. This has the effect of tensing the muscles, consequently inhibiting hand action in the swing. Tense or tight muscles do not work efficiently, and a tight grip slows down the muscles.

A good analogy for grip pressure is to grip the club only as tightly as you would grip a car steering wheel if you were driving at about 40 miles per hour along a smooth, straight road.

Next time you drive, make a mental note of how much pressure you apply to the steering wheel and how, if you tighten your grip it makes the wheel more difficult to control. Try to take your steering wheel grip to the golf course. It is only on shots perhaps from thick rough or some very specialist shots that you might wish to tighten the grip at address.

Only grip the club as you would a car steering wheel if you were driving along a smooth road at about 40 mph.

In the golf swing we need the hands to work very much as a unit and to that end I use and teach the overlapping, or **Vardon** grip, (named after Harry Vardon who popularized it).

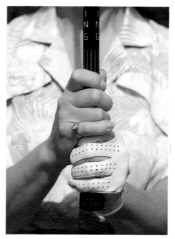

The Vardon grip has the little finger of the right hand overlapping the index and middle fingers of the left.

However, there are two other methods that are acceptable where the hands are placed in the same fashion as with the overlapping grip, but where the position of the right little finger is different.

With the **interlocking** grip the right little finger is interlocked between the index and middle fingers of the left hand. I dislike this grip because I feel it takes some of the control away from the left hand, but several top class players use it most successfully.

The interlocking grip has the little finger of the right hand interlocked with the index finger of the left.

The **baseball** grip is where both hands sit completely on the grip, and is often favoured by younger players, or those with very small hands, but if you use this, be sure that there is no gap between your hands.

Players with smaller hands often use the baseball grip, with all ten fingers on the club.

If you have used either of these grips for some time I would not insist that you change them, providing that your hands are positioned on the grip according to the guidelines given earlier in this chapter. The placement of the hands, rather than the position of the right little finger, is far more crucial to good golf. However, it always pays to experiment a little in this game, and by hitting some shots with the over-lapping grip you may decide to change to what is the most widely used grip in golf.

GRIPS TO AVOID

One of the most common bad grips I see is where the left hand is placed in too weak a position (too far to the left), and the right in too strong a position (too far to the right). This really has nothing to commend it as the hands cannot work together as a unit and usually the left wrist gets very much out of position in the backswing, preventing the hands from developing any power. The shaft of the club does not sit under the pad at the heel of the hand, but too much in the centre of the palm.

If you recognise this when you look in the mirror, **start rebuilding your grip right now**, because whatever ability you may have is going to struggle to manifest itself with this grip.

This is one of the worst grips I see, with the hands pointing in opposite directions. They would work against each other, rather than together. The club also tends to sit more in the palm of the hand, as seen in the inset.

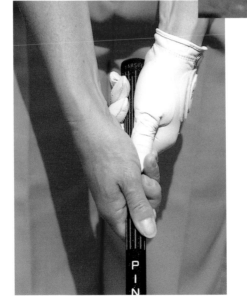

THE STRONG GRIP

When both hands are turned too much to the right, the grip is called strong, and both 'V's will point too much towards the right shoulder, with almost all of the knuckles on the left hand visible. This grip can have one of two effects on the ball, neither of which is desirable. It is quite possible to return the clubface very open to the ball, causing a slice or a shot lacking distance, since the hands are unable to release their power and square the clubface. This is known as blocked hand action.

Alternatively, some players will release their hands into the shot and close the clubface quite severely, thus hooking the ball.

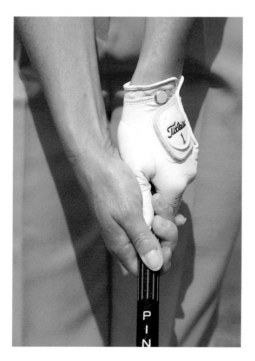

Left: A strong grip has the hands turned too far to the right.

Above right: This can often cause you to return the clubface to the ball in a very open position, causing a slice.

Right: Players who use good hand action might, however, return the clubface to the ball closed, thus hooking it.

The Weak Grip

The Long Thumb

When both hands are turned too much to the left, the grip is called weak, and the 'V's will point too much towards the chin, with probably only one knuckle visible on the left hand. It will cause a fade or slice depending which club you use, and the hands' exact position.

    The hands will not return to their address position at impact, but will be in a more neutral position, where the 'V's point more towards the right side of the face, thus leaving the clubface open.

When the left thumb stretches down the grip it tenses the forearm.

The left thumb should be about level with the forefinger knuckle.

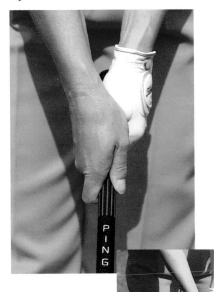

A weak grip has the hands turned too far to the left, which will cause you to return the clubface open at impact.

    No, this is not a physical deformity, but a term applied when the left thumb is stretched down the grip, and is evident more when the grip is weak. It puts the grip too much in the fingers of the left hand stretching the muscles at the front of the forearm, thus rendering them rather useless. It prevents a good release of the clubhead and tends to lead to a less powerful, sliced shot. Check that when you look face on in the mirror, the end of your thumb is virtually level with the forefinger knuckle.

PRACTICE TIPS

Stand in front of a mirror with your hands hanging by your side and you will see that the back of your left hand half faces the mirror; this is how it should be placed on the club.

Without moving the left hand, place a club in it, and you will find that it rests correctly in your slightly curled fingers, and under the heel of your hand.

You may need a friend to help you at first but will soon find this an easy process on your own.

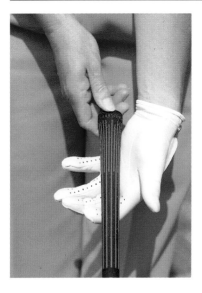
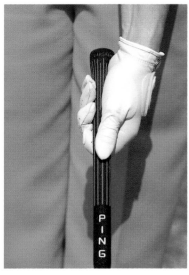
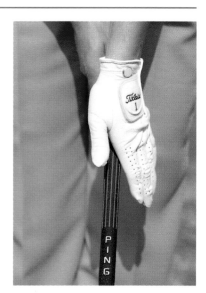

You can even practise sitting in a chair. Hold the club in your right hand where the rubber grip ends so that the shaft is about 60° from the horizontal. Now position your left hand checking that you can see the correct number of knuckles.

You will find that with the shaft held in this manner, it will lie correctly in the left hand. Now simply slide the right hand down until it is in position. As you will have been holding the thinner part of the shaft, you will have held it in the fingers of the right hand, and this will encourage you to use the correct finger grip when you slide the hand down. Even on those dreary winter nights you can sit in the warm comfort of your lounge and improve your golf!

Left: When you bring the left hand onto the grip, don't make the mistake of trying to check the position of the club in this manner, because when you close your fingers around the grip, the hand will be in a very weak position.

Instead, have the left palm facing more towards the right knee, and then the shaft will run under the heel of the hand and not up the centre of the palm.

AIM AND ALIGNMENT

Having gripped the club correctly it is now vital that the whole swing is aimed in the correct direction. Whilst that may sound easy, believe me, even the best players in the world constantly check this aspect of their game because they know that it is easy to misalign both the clubface and the body.

Once this happens then some compensation in the swing must be made if the ball is to finish on target. This is a slippery slope to find oneself on and only serves to make a fairly difficult game even more difficult.

Why is correct alignment so difficult? Unlike many other sports, we do not face our target, but face sideways to it. We do not stand on the line of the target, but stand perhaps two to three feet to the side of it. Ask a marksman to fire his rifle standing in a similar position and he would have a very difficult task in lining up the barrel accurately. This puts our alignment problems into context, and you should not think that you are in a minority if you find this aspect of the game most trying.

Correct aim and alignment are interrelated with the position of the ball. If your alignment, particularly that of your shoulders, is out of position, then the entire swing will be misaimed. The problem is that we are usually not aware how much out of position we may be and often attribute wayward shots purely to a swing fault.

In teaching, the first fundamental of giving a lesson is to check the address position of the pupil, and almost without exception there is something wrong with the aim and the alignment of a player. Often they have no set pre-shot routine to assist them and therefore the whole aiming process becomes rather a lottery.

It is as if the pupil considers this part of golf to be irrelevant, when in fact it is one of the most important aspects. If you watch the top professionals play you will find that whilst the pre-shot routine varies from player to player, each has an unfailingly regular procedure which makes it easy to hit the ball towards the target.

The following procedure, which you can practise at home in front of a mirror, or in the garden, will help you.

Stand behind the ball looking towards the target and pick out a spot on the ground about two to three feet ahead of the ball as an intermediate target. The reason for this is that it is far easier to aim over something close to you than a target perhaps 100 yards away.

Gripping the club stand opposite the ball with your feet together, so that the back of the ball is in line with the inside of your left foot.

Stand behind the ball and pick out an intermediate target a few feet away that you can use to help you align correctly.

With the clubface square, stand with your feet together, the back of the ball in line with the inside of your left foot.

Angle forward from the hips, your knees flexed and your seat out. The shoulders must remain square.

Move your left foot about three inches (the width of your shoe) to the left.

Lower the club to the ground by bending forward from the hips and place the clubface squarely behind the ball. If you can imagine a line extended back from the intermediate target to the ball, this should help you to set the clubface square.

You can see that as I have angled forward, even at this stage my shoulders and hips are parallel to the target line, which is exactly what I want to achieve.

Now move your left foot about three inches to the left, which is roughly the width of your shoe. This will be the position of your left foot for all shots with an iron from flat lies.

The completed stance for a medium iron, the left arm and shaft forming a straight line.

flexed towards each other.

Also, note that the shaft of the club slopes forward (i.e. towards the target) a little, so that the hands are ahead of the ball and the left arm and shaft form a straight line from this viewpoint. Because the right hand is below the left on the grip, so the right shoulder must be lower than the left, and you should feel that your head is behind the ball.

The view down the line best demonstrates what to look for in good alignment. It shows that my shoulders, hips and feet are all parallel to the target line. Whilst the left arm is comfortably straight, the right arm is softer, with the elbow just flexing towards the right hip bone.

Notice that the top part of the left forearm is just visible, which you should be able to check if you set up with a mirror to your right. Remember your shoulders do not aim at the target, but together with the feet and hips are parallel and left of the target.

Your shoulders, hips, knees and feet must be parallel to the target line, your arms hanging freely.

Move your right foot about ten inches to the right, allowing your weight to settle equally on the inside half of each foot. I have given approximate distances, which should be about right for most players, but your height does come into it. You want to feel that your stance is wide enough to give you mobility as well as stability.

If you are hitting a longer iron, widen the stance just a little by moving the right foot further to the right; if you use a short iron, then narrow the stance by moving the right foot not so far to the right.

All the time the left foot keeps the same relevant position to the ball; it is the right foot that builds the width. Both feet can be angled out slightly, but try to feel the weight more towards the inside, and have your knees gently

THE BALL POSITION

When you swing the club it will travel back towards the ball in a downward direction, travel parallel to the ground for a short time, and then swing upwards again.

To hit an iron shot correctly, the ball must be struck when the clubhead is still descending, and so the ball must be positioned opposite your feet accordingly. The guidelines I have already given you should be suitable for most club golfers, but you may need to make slight adjustments so that you get the exact ball/turf contact required.

When you hit a fairway wood, the cleanest contact is made when the clubhead is travelling parallel to the ground, which is the lowest point in the swing, generally called the base of the arc.

Therefore the ball should be played further forward in the stance, about one inch nearer the left heel. When you stand with your feet together opposite the ball, move your left foot about two inches to the left.

Shots with a 3-wood or driver from a tee peg should be struck when the club has just started to ascend, so the ball must be positioned opposite your feet at the relevant point.

For this your left foot should not be moved as far left as for a fairway wood, so that the ball is about an inch inside your left heel. With the ball this far forward it is easy to fall into the trap of letting the right side stretch forwards, thus causing the shoulders to aim to the left. Instead, try to feel that the right shoulder has lowered more than when hitting an iron. Also, set a little more weight on the right foot, about 55–60%. The stance is now at its widest, but do be careful that it does not get so wide that it hampers your ability to transfer your weight during the swing.

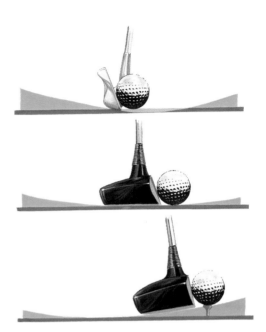

To hit an iron correctly the club should still be descending. For a fairway wood the best contact is made when the clubhead is travelling parallel to the ground.
For a driver from the tee the clubhead is just beginning to rise as it hits the ball.

Above left: The ball is positioned about two inches inside the left heel for a fairway wood. To show the ball position better in this picture I have just teed it up very slightly.

Above right: For the driver the ball is positioned about an inch inside the left heel.

BALL TOO FAR FORWARD

When the ball is placed too far forward in the stance, it will inevitably pull your shoulders into an open position, and this means that your swing will be aimed to the left creating an out-to-in swing path, which will cause you to slice, pull and top shots.

With the ball too far forward the shoulders become open.

With the ball too far back the shoulders become closed.

SHOULDERS OPEN

Even with the ball correctly positioned, many players manage to get their shoulders open.

This is generally caused by keeping the right arm too straight, which brings the right shoulder forward. This can cause a slice, pull, or a topped shot.

BALL TOO FAR BACK

This is a much less common fault, but has an influence on the set-up and swing. It will cause the shoulders to aim too far to the right in a closed position, generally creating a swing path too much from the inside.

It tends to prevent the weight moving onto the left foot at impact, the weight remaining on the right side and the player trying to hit the ball in an upward fashion. It can cause shots that are pushed or hooked, as well as totally mis-hit.

If the right arm is too straight the shoulders will be in an open position.

PRACTICE TIPS

To help you judge the correct ball position and alignment, lay two clubs on the ground parallel to the target line, and a third placed so that it shows you exactly where the ball is in relation to your feet. If you practice in this manner, put a couple of tee pegs in to show your feet position, then walk round so that you stand opposite the ball. This will give you a better perspective of your set-up.

If your shoulders are in an open position and you have great trouble in squaring them, try addressing the ball as follows.

Grip the club in your left hand only, keeping your right arm by your side. In this way, with the left side only stretched forward, your right side cannot be so dominant.

Now place your right hand on the grip, taking great care not to let the right shoulder come forward too much. Keep the right elbow soft and, if anything, feel that the right wrist is slightly arched. In the correct position your right shoulder will feel lower than usual and you will feel that your shoulders are aimed to the right.

Always check your position in a mirror, both face on and from the rear. Put this book on the floor beside you, and compare your address position to mine.

POSTURE

This is one of the least understood aspects of the set-up, but one of the most important, so let me explain first what we mean by posture.

It refers to the angles of the head, spine and knees, and also to the weight distribution.

So why is it important? Golf is played by incorporating certain different movements of the entire body.

Whilst the alignment of the body dictates the line of the swing, so the posture dictates whether certain parts of the body, particularly the hips and shoulders, are going to move correctly. It sets the distance from the ball and has the greatest influence on the angle that we swing the club, called the swing plane. Don't worry too much about this phrase for now because, if the posture is correct, it will encourage the correct movements in the swing.

Attaining correct posture seems more difficult for ladies than men, and I believe I know why.

When adopting correct posture, it requires the lower part of the spine to be very slightly hollowed out, thus pushing the seat out behind you. This tilts the pelvis backwards, when for most of our lives we have been taught, particularly in any deportment classes, to keep the seat tucked under, pelvis forwards.

For ladies suddenly to be told to stick their seats out goes against the grain. I assure you that it feels worse than it looks; in fact I would be amazed if anyone really noticed, but it will enable you to swing the club in a better fashion.

Good posture shows my back straight, seat out, knees flexed, weight more towards the balls of my feet and my chin up.

To attain correct posture stand with the club held out horizontally in front of you, with the top part of your arms, from shoulder to elbow, lightly touching the sides of your body.

Now angle forward from the hips, keeping the spine straight, and allow your seat to go out behind you. Put your feet apart and lightly flex your knees. This will help set you the correct distance from the ball.

With the shaft horizontal, angle forward from the hips to lower the club to the ground.

Notice that, although from face-on the left arm and shaft should form virtually a straight line, from down the line there must be an angle between your arms and the shaft.

You will find that much of your weight will be on the balls of your feet, though some of course, must be on the heels.

The head must remain an extension of the spine, as it is when you are standing normally. Do not let the phrase, 'keep your head down', cause you to have your chin almost on your chest. If this happens you will have great difficulty making a good shoulder turn.

Because the lower part of the spine is slightly hollowed out, the back has a fairly straight, rather than rounded look to it.

This method of getting the correct posture is suitable for all clubs. If you use a driver, because it has a longer shaft, the clubhead will touch the ground sooner as you bend forward, so the spine will be more upright and your distance from the ball greater.

When using a short iron, the forward angle of the spine increases and you will stand closer to the ball. Notice also that the gap between the hands and the legs decreases with the shorter irons.

That, then, is how to adopt the correct posture at the ball. On the next two pages you will see some of the more common faults that are encountered in this department of the game.

If you can avoid them, perhaps after even recognising them in your own set-up, you will be doing yourself a big favour.

The spine is more upright when using the driver as this club has the longest shaft.

The spine is angled forward more for a wedge and the ball played closer to the feet, because the shaft is shorter.

FAULTS TO AVOID

Below is a rather rounded looking address position I see all too often. In this instance the seat has been tucked under, and the weight is on the heels. It will be impossible for the body to turn correctly out of the way in the back swing, and usually this leads to an overly upright arm swing. Loss of power and accuracy will result.

Often as a result of the previous fault, the player senses that the arms have no room in which to swing and therefore tries to create this space by arching the wrists. Correct wrist action is now a forlorn hope, and therefore your true potential will never be reached. Weak and poorly struck shots will be commonplace.

This position (**opposite, right**) can also be caused when the player tries to rest the whole of the sole of the club on the ground. In the correct address position about a quarter of the sole at the toe end should be clear of the ground. If this is not evident when you adopt correct posture then it would be worth asking your club professional to check the lie of your clubs.

For the total beginner this element is not vitally important, but when you buy a set of clubs this should be checked. There is more information about this point on page 154.

This is a less common fault where, because the ball is played too far away from the golfer, the spine has to be angled too far forward. The result is a swing where the body and arms can not swing in a coordinated fashion. The arms can either swing very flat, or in perhaps less severe examples the shoulders turn too steeply. Please believe me neither option is desirable.

This is almost good, but in an effort to feel comfortable and stable the weight has been moved too much towards the heels, and the knees have flexed too much. Whilst it will give a feeling of stability at address, it will deny the player enough mobility, and the legs will not be used correctly. There is a saying in golf that you should feel as if you are sitting on a shooting stick, but when doing this, much of the weight will be on the heels, which you want to avoid at address. So keep this saying and the picture it conjures up, out of your mind.

PRACTICE TIPS

The best tip I know is to practise the method I have shown you in front of a mirror.

If you have, in the past, had too much weight on your heels, and your seat tucked under (which is by far the most common fault I see), with the correct posture you will feel very strange at first, as if you are about to topple forwards. At address you should be able to move each heel in turn up and down. This would not be possible with too much weight on the heels.

To give you a better idea of how good posture should feel, imagine that you are about to dive into a swimming pool, or jump forwards, and you would have to put your weight more towards the front of your feet and would angle your spine forwards. This is more the feeling to strive for.

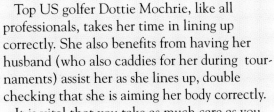

Stand upright holding a club shaft behind you so that is touches your spine and lightly touches your head. Now angle forward from your hips keeping the shaft touching those parts and you will get a feeling of keeping your back straight and your head up.

Top US golfer Dottie Mochrie, like all professionals, takes her time in lining up correctly. She also benefits from having her husband (who also caddies for her during tournaments) assist her as she lines up, double checking that she is aiming her body correctly.

It is vital that you take as much care as you possibly can in getting this vital part of golf correct.

THE SWING

Before I explain in detail what ought to be happening in a good golf swing, I would like to give you an overall picture of this action. As a beginner the whole process can feel like a series of different movements rather than one flowing action, and initially this is inevitable.

As you progress one movement blends subconsciously into another and you begin to feel the rhythm of the swing as the weight transfers back and through. Despite the fact that we stand in a stationary position, hitting a golf ball has many similarities to propelling other objects forwards.

This is not always evident and we tend to become much more rigid when trying to hit a golf ball than, say, throwing a ball or playing a tennis shot. I will give you some good analogies which hopefully will help you to understand how a golf swing should feel.

The best players swing using the entire body, but unfortunately many club golfers rely solely on their hands and arms to hit the ball.

This is why the set-up is so important because, when you stand correctly, all parts of your body are capable of contributing to the swing.

Let me describe the swing in fairly simple terms: you are trying to swing the club in a circle around a fixed point at the top of the spine. In the backswing your body must turn as your arms swing the club upwards.

As your arms swing the club down, your body will turn back so that at impact you are almost back in your address position. Once the ball is struck, the arms swing upwards as the body turns through to face the target.

During the backswing the weight must transfer to the right foot, and back onto the left foot by the completion of the swing. The wrists will cock and uncock at impact in such a manner

that creates power. So, in very simplistic terms, the body provides the inward element of the swing while the arms provide the up and down element. Of course these movements have to be coordinated and timed, but I hope that this gives you a basic picture of what you are trying to do.

Earlier, I explained the movement of the clubhead, and as you learn to play golf, or try to improve your swing, it will help you either to focus on what the clubhead is doing, or, alternatively to feel and see what your body is doing. Different thoughts work for different people at different times.

Whilst you may feel that you swing the clubhead back towards 3.30, a friend may try to concentrate on moving her left shoulder and arm away from the ball. You will both end up with the same movement, achieved in different ways, but whatever thought produces the correct movement is right for you at that time.

Beth Daniel, the 1990 LPGA champion, captured on camera just after impact. As she swings through her hands release the clubhead, creating a crisp shot.

The art of teaching golf is to be able to say the same thing in different ways, and I will describe what is happening both to the clubhead and to the entire body. So let's look at the swing in detail, but remember that although I am breaking the swing down into many parts, it is really one continuous, flowing movement.

THE BACKSWING

The backswing is started by a combined movement of the left shoulder, arm, shaft and clubhead away from the ball.

The hands remain passive at this stage, so that the club has initially stayed low to the ground moving towards 3 o'clock, then gently inwards towards 3.30. The right hip has started to move backwards just a little, while the left knee has flexed inwards.

When the hands have reached waist height the wrists have started to cock, so there is an angle between the shaft and the left arm. The shoulders and hips have continued turning but

As the hands reach waist height the right elbow folds, the left remaining comfortably straight.

note that the shoulders have turned more than the hips. The arms have rotated slightly clockwise, but the left arm is still comfortably straight while the right elbow has started to fold downwards. The back of the left hand and palm of the right are parallel to the target line The head remains steady, eyes focused on the ball.

The clubhead has continued its inward and upward path and the clubface is square to the horizon, with the toe in the air. The right knee retains its original flex as weight starts to increase on this side.

When the top of the backswing is reached, the shoulders have turned approximately 90° and the hips 45°. The left arm is still comfortably straight, though **not absolutely straight** as this would cause too much tension.

The right elbow has continued to fold and now points downwards. The right knee still keeps its flex, while the left points just behind the ball.

Whilst I manage to make this movement keeping my left heel almost on the ground it is quite in order to let yours rise just a little at the last moment if this helps you to make a full turn. Flexibility will vary from player to player.

The arms and shoulders move away as a unit, whilst the hands remain passive.

Ideally the shaft will be parallel to the target line and horizontal. The clubface is square, which means it is parallel to the back of the left forearm. The wrists are fully cocked so that there is an angle of 90° between the left arm and the shaft.

The wrists have cocked so that at this point the left thumb is in a supportive position under the shaft; the left wrist has cocked so that the thumb moves towards the inside of the forearm.

The right wrist has cocked so that the back of the hand has moved slightly towards the top part of the forearm, the palm now half facing the sky.

One of the most important points to note is that I have retained the spinal angle set at address so that my head, despite turning slightly to the right to allow a good shoulder turn, has remained at the same height. Because of good posture my right side has turned quite readily out of the way as my arms have swung upwards.

The majority of weight is now on the right side, being retained on the inside and centre of the right foot, with a noticeable increase of weight on the right heel.

In the simple description of the swing we have now reached the point where the body has turned to the right while the arms have swung the club up.

The clubhead swings gradually inside. When the hands are at waist height the clubface is square to the horizontal.

At the top of the backswing the shoulders have turned 90°, the hips about 45°. The club shaft is horizontal and parallel to the target line, with the clubface square. The weight is mainly on the right foot with the right knee flexed.

THE CHANGE OF DIRECTION

This is one of the crucial parts of the swing, when even a good backswing can be ruined if the correct sequence of movements does not take place. At the top of the backswing there is a distinct feeling of coiling the top half of the body against the resistance of the lower half, so that power is developed. At the start of the downswing we must preserve most of that power for when we need it (i.e. at impact) and in order to do that, the lower half of the body (i.e. the legs and hips) must move before the top half of the body.

The left knee moves towards the target as the weight transfers smoothly to the left.

Slow motion cameras would show us that as the shoulders and arms are completing their backward journey, the legs are already starting

the downswing. How much each player senses this happening varies depending on what you are focusing on in the swing, but I believe that if you can have the picture of starting your arms down at the same time as the weight starts to transfer back to the left side then you will not go far wrong. This will keep a sense of tautness in the swing that is felt at the completion of the correct backswing.

The arms swing the club down on the inside as the hips begin to square up.

THE DOWNSWING

At the start of my downswing you can see that my left leg has moved towards the target and that my hips are starting to return to a square position. The shoulders have moved only a short distance in response to this leg action and to the fact that my left arm is pulling downwards. The arms have dropped into the space created when the right side of my body turned out of the way in the backswing. It is clearly visible that the clubhead is now approaching from inside the target line and that most of the angle between my left arm and the shaft has been retained. My head is still behind the ball.

As the downswing progresses so more weight is transferred back onto the left foot and the hips continue to turn so that they start to open to the target. The club is now approaching from the 3.30 direction and the right hand is still in a slightly cocked position, ready to release its power.

IMPACT

At impact the shoulders are virtually square (i.e. almost parallel to the target line) with the hips in an open position. The arms are back almost as they were at address and the wrists have now straightened as the hands strike the ball. The left knee is still flexed as the weight transfers to that side and the right knee moves towards the left knee. The eyes are fully focused on the ball and the posture has been retained so that the head is still at the same height. The clubface is now square, so the ball will fly straight at the target.

At impact the hands release their power and square the clubface.

The clubhead approaches from the 3.30 direction as the hips are opening to the target.

THE FOLLOW THROUGH

Just after impact the hands and arms start to rotate anti-clockwise as the right hand and arm extend towards the target. As a result the clubhead swings back inside the target line and the clubface closes to this line. The body is pulled through by the arms as the weight continues to flow onto the left side. The right knee moves in sympathy as the heel fully releases from the ground, but the head keeps its impact position as much as possible. The original posture is kept as a safeguard against the body and head lifting and causing poor contact with the ball.

At waist height the hands and arms have continued their rotation, so that the toe of the club is in the air and the back of the right and

The clubhead swings back inside the target line as the clubface closes to it. The posture is maintained.

The right hand rotates over the left as the right knee moves towards the target.

palm of the left hand are virtually parallel to the target line. The left elbow is now folding downwards while the wrists cock upwards again. There is a great similarity between this position and that in the backswing when the hands are also waist height. Only now does the head begin to turn towards the target as the body continues to turn through.

At the completion of the swing the body and hips have turned through to face just left of the target, and the head, which is now above the left foot, faces the target. Almost all of the weight is now on the outside and heel of the left foot, with only the tips of the toes of the right foot in contact with the ground. The spinal angle is slightly more upright, but by the time this happens the ball is well on its way.

The arms have swung upwards over the left shoulder so that the club hangs down behind my head. This is a balanced position attained by swinging through the ball, not at the ball.

Having read through this section please do

At waist height the toe of the club is in the air. When the swing is completed your head is above the left foot, your weight almost entirely on that side.

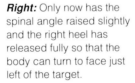

Right: Only now has the spinal angle raised slightly and the right heel has released fully so that the body can turn to face just left of the target.

not think that what I have written is what I think about when I am swinging. I have merely described what happens, in my case perfectly naturally. If I thought about too many things at once, any natural ability and the free flowing elements of the swing would be hampered.

I tend to know what my swing faults are and would perhaps, therefore, have one or, at most, two swing thoughts when I play, but like every-one else I have gradually built my swing over many years so that the component parts have improved and have become natural. When I practise, I concentrate on a specific movement that I wish to change, but it all takes time and patience.

BUILDING THE SWING

If you are a complete beginner at golf I would advise you to limit the length of your swing so that your hands only swing back to a point just beyond waist height in the backswing and perhaps a little further on the through swing. It is difficult at first to control the club sufficiently to make a full backswing, and contact with the ball will most likely be quite poor and sometimes even non-existent!

Most people I have taught from the beginning have wanted to hit the ball straight away, which is quite understandable, but as a teacher I really want them to concentrate on how to swing. Using a ball can distract you.

It is best to work at first without any particular target, then to try to hit a tee peg or a leaf. Although these are quite small objects, any contact will move them, whereas when hitting a golf ball it is really only correct contact that will get the ball airborne. When hitting the ball, sit it up on a tee peg, so that your task is made easier; success will encourage you.

The correct body action in the golf swing will be possible because of good posture and set-up, but as it cannot be guaranteed, it is a good idea to practise this movement in isolation.

Stand with a club held across the back of your shoulders. Keeping your spine upright flex your knees and stick your seat out slightly. Now turn to the right, keeping your eyes focused ahead.

Your shoulders will turn about 90°, your hips 45° and this is the same action as in the backswing, the only difference being that your spine will be angled forwards. Turn through to the left so that you finish facing the target with your right heel off the ground.

Now let's take this a stage further. Keeping the club in place, angle forward from the hips so that you adopt your address position with your seat pushed out behind you slightly. Turn your shoulders 90° to the right so that the shaft points out in front of you.

Create that same turning action with the shoulders and body as before. Keep the angle in

Stand with a club behind your shoulders and turn to the right as you would in the backswing.

Angle forward from the hips, with your seat out, as in the address position.

the right knee and feel that you turn around this knee with your weight moving onto the right foot as well. I should make it clear that although the right knee retains its flex, the knee itself will move from a point above the inside of the right foot to a position above the centre of that foot, so some lateral movement will occur.

Many lady golfers incorrectly straighten the right knee in the backswing, but using this drill you will be more likely to do the correct thing and retain the flex.

Focus on a spot on the ground where the ball might be and you will then start to feel how

It is very important to retain the forward angle of the spine.

By turning to the right and then to the left you will start to feel how your body should work in the golf swing. Retain the right knee flex on the backswing and release the right heel as you swing through.

your body should work in the backswing. You will feel a stretching sensation around your back, providing you keep the left heel down or close to the ground if you are not very flexible.

Now turn back to the left so that you finish facing the target with your right heel off the ground. For the purposes of this exercise, retain your posture so that your head and eyes are at an angle.

By doing this exercise in two stages you will fully appreciate how the shoulders must turn rather than tilt. Repeat it from the erect spine position, so that you get a definite feeling of turning back and through. You will also feel how the weight transference takes place. It is a natural movement at this stage and it is only when we have a club in our hands that it tends to become inhibited.

Of course this exercise can be done without a club behind your back and I would suggest that you repeat it whenever possible. It will help condition the back muscles as well as train them to make the correct movements.

THE ARM ACTION

I have already stated that, in simple terms, the body provides the turning element in the swing, and the arms the up and down element. The previous exercise will, I am sure, make you very aware of the body's job, so now let's look at the role of the arms.

Take the address position without a club, your arms hanging in what is a very relaxed manner. They should feel fairly heavy as they hang, while your legs should feel quite lively and springy. Open your hands keeping the palms about two to three inches apart.

I now want you to make the backswing by turning the body, but thinking of swinging your arms upwards. Again, if you can stand with a mirror to your right, look in it as you swing back to check this action. Without a club it is easy to feel what your arms must do. Try to keep the palms a constant distance apart, the left arm fairly straight, but the right one folding.

Now swing your arms back down to where they started in the address position and you will definitely feel the correct up and down motion that is required.

Repeat this several times, then continue the swing through to the finish. In this instance, as your body turns through to face the target, your arms will swing upwards again, the left will fold and the right elbow will also soften.

Do be careful that as you swing you do not stretch your arms away from the shoulder joints in the backswing. The very top part of the left arm should be touching the chest.

This simple exercise will give you a good idea of how the swing should feel and indeed the swinging aspect of the movement should become very obvious.

However, we need to take this a stage further in order to be certain that the correct movements are being made. I want you to swing back and stop your hands at waist height.

Check that your forearms have rotated very slightly clockwise and the palm of the right hand, and back of the left hand are parallel to the target line, with the right elbow beginning to fold.

Now swing to the corresponding point on the through swing. If you have made the movement correctly the forearms will have rotated anti-clockwise so the palm of the left hand and back of the right are once again parallel to the target line, with the left elbow beginning to fold.

At waist height check that the palm of your right, and back of your left hands are parallel to the target.

At the corresponding height on the through swing the hands are again parallel to the target line.

Whether you are a complete beginner or a more experienced player, use this drill to check your swing. By swinging without a club you will get a better sensation of the exact movements in the swing.

With your arms hanging relaxed, swing them up, down, then up again as the body turns back and through.

THE HAND ACTION

We have looked at the action of two of the main components in the golf swing; now we must deal with the vital part played by the hands. I will assume that you are gripping the club correctly. If you have any doubts, do take time to refresh your memory by re-reading the grip section on pages 14–23.

With a club, take your address position; then, keeping your arms still, cock your wrists upwards so that the shaft is just above the horizontal. This is the direction in which your wrists will hinge during the backswing. You will see wrinkles have appeared at the base of the left thumb and towards the back of the right hand. For this exercise it would be best if you do not wear a golf glove.

Without moving your arms cock your wrists up in front of you so that the shaft is horizontal. Check for the wrinkles at the base of your left thumb.

Now swing your arms back so that your hands are at waist height, allowing the right elbow to fold slightly. You will find that, once again, the palm of the right hand and back of the left are parallel to the target line and the clubface is square to the horizontal, but look carefully at the wrist joints and you find that some of the wrinkles on the left wrist have disappeared.

This is due to the slight rotation of the forearms in the backswing, but when you complete the backswing the wrist cocking will be completed and the wrinkles will become more defined, as the photograph below shows.

All the time this action takes place, notice that the back of the left hand, the back of the left forearm, and the clubface remain parallel to each other, which in golfing terms is called square. By moving your wrists in this fashion you will find it easier to hit the ball straight without excessive manipulation by the hands.

Above: Keeping the wrists cocked swing your arms back to waist height, letting the right elbow fold slightly.

Below: At the top check for the wrinkles at the base of the left thumb created by the correct wrist action. The left thumb sits under the shaft.

Go back to the address position, cock the wrists up in front of you again, then swing through to waist height and you will be in the correct position with the palm of the left hand and back of the right parallel to the target line and the clubface square to the horizontal.

This, then, explains the direction in which the wrists cock during the swing, and is an action which takes place gradually once the hands have passed the right thigh. Whilst the beginner may feel this as a conscious movement, providing the grip is sound the wrists will cock naturally in response to the swinging weight of the clubhead. Remember, it is the arms and the body which start the back-swing, the hands initially remaining passive before starting to cock in an upwards fashion.

When the wrists cock correctly the back of the left forearm, back of the left hand and the clubface remain virtually parallel to one another.

At waist height on the through swing the wrists cock upwards, almost a mirror image of the backswing.

PUTTING IT ALL TOGETHER

Having looked at the various component parts of the swing, we now need to put them back together.

I will divide this into two parts, the first for the complete beginner, the second for the more experienced player who, nevertheless may learn something from reading the beginners' section.

THE BEGINNER

Work through the exercises that have been detailed so far, but limit the length of your swing so that at first the hands stop at about waist height in the backswing and through swing. Make plenty of swings without a ball so that you just get used to holding and swinging the club, as well as standing correctly.

Stop on some of the backswings to check the alignment of your hands and the clubface, and try to hold the through swing position to confirm that you are balanced correctly. You will find it helpful to lay a couple of clubs on the ground parallel to your target line to assist with alignment, as the photograph below shows.

You will find it useful to lay clubs on the ground to help with your alignment.

Once this movement starts to feel a little more natural, let the backswing extend slightly so that your hands reach about shoulder height.

As you swing through try to accelerate the clubhead through the impact zone and then hold your balance at the end of the swing. You should get the feeling of swishing the clubhead. This will only happen if you do not grip too tightly.

If you start to sense tension in your hands and forearms, then remember the steering wheel analogy and regrip, placing the hands lightly on the club.

A good drill to help you get the feeling of the swing is to hold the club in the air with the clubhead about shoulder height. Keep the top part of each arm from shoulder to elbow lightly touching the sides of your body and swing, keeping the head of the club the same height throughout the swing. This is best done where you can see your reflection.

In order to do this correctly the right elbow must fold in the backswing and your arms must rotate clockwise. The left elbow must fold in the through swing as the arms now rotate anti-clockwise. You will find that, providing you have your knees flexed and your seat out, your body will turn fairly naturally in response to your arm swing. Try to make the clubhead accelerate as it passes your nose.

This in essence is the golf swing action, but the difference is that in the golf swing the clubhead is lowered to the ground by angling the spine forward.

Once you have swung horizontally a few times, angle your spine forwards so that the clubhead is about two feet off the ground and repeat the exercise. Your arms will now swing a little more upright, but you should have the same feeling of turning the body as you swing the arms up.

Next, angle the spine forward sufficiently so that the club rests on the ground, and then swing. Your arms must now swing more upright, but still allow the right elbow to fold in the backswing and the left in the through swing.

I would not expect you to contact the ball accurately at this stage, so make plenty of swings, just trying to hit perhaps a leaf, tee-peg, or simply brush the grass opposite your stance.

One of the major problems in the swing is trying to coordinate the turn as well as swing the arms. What generally happens is that the arms collapse and are hugged into the body, a fault that is referred to as 'losing width in the swing'.

If the arms are not extended to their original address position at impact, the radius of the circle is narrowed and the ball can be missed altogether, or be hit off the toe of the club, shooting violently to the right.

The best way to eliminate this fault is to keep

Stand with the club in the air and swing, keeping the clubhead at the same height, letting the right elbow fold on the backswing, and the left on the through swing. Then lower the clubhead to the ground and repeat this exercise.

the left arm as straight as you can without either stretching it away from the shoulder or keeping it ramrod stiff. As you swing your arms down have the feeling of straightening them at impact, and this will help you to recover your address position.

When you practise do hit some balls, but spend at least two-thirds of your practice time aiming at a leaf or an imaginary ball.

As you progress you will find that you can extend your swing so that it becomes full length, but any time your contact becomes very bad, go back to the half swing and gradually build up again.

Many ladies swing the club back too far and lose control of it. The length of swing of the world's top players does vary, but in all cases they have control of the club. As a guideline, swinging the shaft to a horizontal position or just past it would be ideal, but if you start to see the club out of your left eye at the end of the backswing then you have probably swung too far. Always check that you have not loosened the last three fingers of the left hand, or have excessively bent the left arm.

If you swing back too fast, then you are more likely to lose control. Once you have become accustomed to swinging then the pace of the swing can be increased without loss of control.

Above: Letting go with the last three fingers of the left hand will cause a loss of control.

Below: This is a good turn but the left arm has collapsed causing a long, uncontrolled swing.

Because the turn is incomplete the swing has lost its width as the arms collapse.

THE EXPERIENCED GOLFER

Having read this far you may have become aware of certain deficiencies in your swing, and on an individual basis these aspects must be corrected. I will deal later with some of the most common faults, but for now I want to give you an overall swing concept.

I would suggest that, as with the beginner, many swings are made without a ball, which does encourage a less inhibited action.

Remember that the point of the backswing is to position the club in such a manner that it will return quite readily to the ball from that 3.30 direction with the clubface square to the target.

The ball is not hit on the backswing but many ladies make a backswing that is too fast, indeed, often faster than the downswing. If you intend making what is the most technically correct backswing you can, it involves using the larger muscles of the back, which will not move as quickly as those in the hands and arms. Logically, the backswing can only be made at the pace of the slowest muscles, which are those of the back and shoulders. Take your pace from these and you will improve your tempo.

So swing back smoothly, allowing the weight to gather on the right foot. **Do not worry about keeping your head still.** It is important that your head stays at the same height, and that it remains steady, but if you concentrate solely on keeping it still, you will inhibit a good turn. Let it rotate slightly to the right so that you look at the ball more with the left eye at the top of the backswing. From this point on, for the good golfer, much of what happens is purely subconscious as they accelerate through to the finish. The club golfer would do well to remember that it is the clubhead that will hit the ball. Most ladies lack clubhead speed, so once the downswing begins create that swishing feeling by throwing the clubhead past the ball with a combined hand and arm action.

This should not be an uncontrolled throwing action, so let me give you an analogy.

Imagine a child's swing; once it has stopped swinging back, it starts to swing down so that it is gradually accelerating towards its fastest point which coincides with its lowest point, before swinging up again and slowing down.

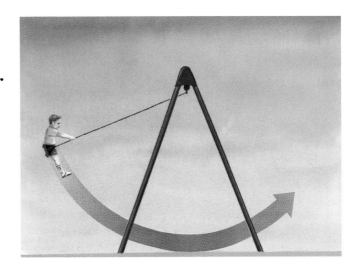

Imagine that the swing gradually accelerates from the top, just like a child's swing.

The golf swing is the same. It is a gradual and smooth acceleration back to the ball from the top of the backswing.

As I mentioned for our beginners, if your grip is too tight you will inhibit the acceleration and try to over-control the club, so keep the grip light but firm, and have the sense of accelerating through to a balanced finish.

During the swing let your weight flow from being even at address onto the right side, then back onto the left.

Check that the clubhead follows the prescribed path, which is made easier by laying a second club down just outside the ball, parallel to the target line. Should you hit this shaft at any time that should ring a warning bell that something is wrong with the swing path.

TIMING AND TEMPO

Getting the timing right for the various move-ments in the swing can be frustrating. Even to the professional player, there are some days when the golf swing feels like one simple flowing movement, and other days when it feels less fluid. The moments at which certain actions take place are critical and because we are using such a small clubhead and a small target only 1.68 inches in diameter, it does not take much inaccuracy to hit a poor shot.

I have already mentioned that the tempo of the backswing should be taken at the pace of the slowest muscles, so that the body has time to turn. The same process is true in the down-swing, where the large thigh and hip muscles make the initial movements. By not rushing the start of the downswing these can duly play their initiating role, followed by those of the arms and hands. But should you quicken the change of direction, there is every chance that the legs will not play their part. Instead the upper body will be too dominant, causing the clubhead to be thrown off line, also resulting in a loss of power.

For the more experienced players who may swing the club making these correct move-ments but perhaps at slightly the wrong time in the swing, see if the following improves your shots.

If you fade, slice or hit thin shots, your legs may be moving too soon and too aggressively in the swing, so concentrate on starting back to the ball with less leg action, and a stronger arm swing.

If you hit strong draw shots, hooked shots, and some fat shots, try making a stronger movement with your left knee and hip to start the downswing.

If your problem is that you are hitting fat shots or hooks you may not be using your legs aggressively enough.

If your legs move too aggressively you will hit fades, slices and thin shots.

Of course timing and tempo are related and the player who swings in a smooth, unhurried manner has a much better chance of achieving the correct timing in her swing. This does not mean that everyone should swing very slowly,

By hitting some mid-iron shots at different speeds you will find your best swing tempo.

One of the tried and tested routines is to hit fifteen 6-iron shots at what feels your natural pace, then hit fifteen more at a slightly increased pace, and fifteen at a slightly slower pace. You will find that one particular pace gives you the best results, taking into consideration length and accuracy.

The other occasion when good tempo seems to be evident is when, instead of trying to hit a fairway wood or long iron very hard in order to carry a hazard, you decide to lay up short of it.

So often in that instance the backswing becomes more leisurely, and everything just slots into place in a very smooth and unhurried manner. The result is that the ball goes further than usual because it was hit in a less frantic manner. Of course the thought then crosses your mind: why didn't you attempt to carry it after all? Well, if you had done, the same type of swing would not have been used, and the effort to hit the ball hard would have seen a different result.

Try to watch women professionals whenever you can, because by seeing their rhythm you can then keep that in mind, mimic it to a great extent, and definitely improve your swing.

as one's personal characteristics have some bearing on the subject. You only have to look at the top women professionals to see that they do not all swing at the same pace.

So, how can you find your best tempo?

If you have the opportunity try to watch women professionals on the practice ground at a tournament. Note how they work through the bag and how they carefully check their alignment and grip before swinging. Their smooth rhythm should be kept in mind.

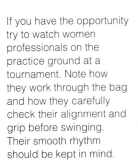

SOME COMMON SWING FAULTS AND CURES

FAULT

The wrists are capable of moving in almost every direction, and initially many beginners have trouble cocking them correctly. Many of them, at waist height, have the left wrist in a very bowed position, where the back of the hand points half downwards, instead of being parallel to the target line. In turn this means the clubface is closed, pointing too much towards the ground instead of being square to the horizontal. Good shots become impossible. This type of action also leads to a short backswing as the upper part of the right arm becomes jammed up against the body.

CURE

Check that the left hand grip shows at least two to two-and-a-half knuckles, then practise, at first without a club, getting the palms parallel to the target line. You need to create more clockwise forearm rotation as you swing back, so that the toe of the club points to the sky.

FAULT

This is almost the opposite of the previous fault, but here the forearms have rotated excessively rolling the clubface open. It is generally caused by a lack of coordinated shoulder and arm movement.

CURE

Set up with the grip end of the club touching your body, gripping down the shaft. Swing back until your hands pass your right leg, keeping the club in place, and you will feel the correct movement for the start of the backswing.
   Once you can do this, when the hands pass the right leg you should have the feeling of working the wrists upwards, so that the thumbs are starting to point skywards, rather than behind you. Reread the hand action section.

FAULT

Although this may look correct (the clubface and hands seem fine) the arms have been swung incorrectly.

This can be proved quite easily and is a very simple way for you to test your swing. Turn your feet and hips round to the right 90°, then lower the club to the ground. (I turned to face the camera.) If the swing is correct, the club will be back in your address position. You can see that in this instance it is well out of position, and proves I have swung back outside the line, i.e. in the 2.30 to 3 o'clock direction.

The same would be true if I had swung my arms too much inside, towards 4 o'clock, except this time the club would sit too far back in my stance when I turned and lowered it.

CURE

Set up with a second club on the ground outside your right foot, parallel to the target line. Swing the club back until it is horizontal, at which point it should be parallel to the one on the ground.

If the shaft points off line one way or the other, this indicates your fault.

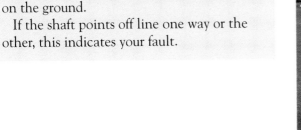

FAULT

When the posture is wrong, with the seat tucked under, the hips will not turn readily and this prevents the shoulders turning as well. The result is that instead of the right hip moving backwards, it moves only laterally to the right with the weight moving onto the outside of the right foot, and the arms get drawn into the body. Good contact is impossible.

CURE

First correct your posture, then do the turning drill on pages 44–45. To help with the new hip movement, imagine that someone is holding your right pocket, pulling it backwards. When you swing you must keep the left arm extended more, so you maintain the width in the swing. Do not stretch the arm from the shoulder joint, but keep the elbow straighter, though not stiff.

FAULT

The arms have been swung up excessively, causing a steep swing plane. This means that the club will descend on the ball from too steep an angle, and too much of the power is therefore directed downwards, and not in propelling the ball forwards. It usually means that the swing path is too much in the 2 o'clock–8 o'clock direction, which leads to a lack of distance. The arms have stretched away from the body too much at the shoulder joint.

CURE

First check that the shaft is parallel to the target line when it is horizontal and if that proves to be the fault then work on this part of the swing. However, sometimes the arms are lifted upwards too much later in the swing, and some of my pupils who have this problem get good results by keeping the upper part of the right arm close to their side during the backswing.

To help you to get the correct feeling, place a head cover or towel under your right armpit, and swing, keeping it in place. This makes you swing flatter and, while it exaggerates this feeling, once the head cover is taken away, you are more likely to produce the correct arm swing.

FAULT

This is the opposite problem to the previous one, where the arms have swung incorrectly, but this time too flat, hugging the body, and losing the up and down element in the swing.

The clubhead approaches too much from the inside, from the 4 o'clock direction and many poor shots can result including pushes, pulls, and topped shots.

CURE

Check that the shaft is parallel to the target line when horizontal. If it is, then from the halfway back position have the feeling of moving the arms upwards above your head, and not backwards behind your head. Picture the right arm, between your shoulder and elbow creating a space between it and your side at the top of the backswing.

FAULT

The right leg has straightened, and it will be difficult to get the correct leg action on the downswing. Instead the top half of the body is used to initiate the downswing, throwing the club onto a steep outside path, creating powerless cut and sliced shots.

CURE

Check your posture, and practise the turning drill on pages 44–45, then hit plenty of half shots concentrating on keeping the original flex in the right knee, making the weight move gently onto the left leg as you swing down.

FAULT

This is the dreaded reverse pivot, where the weight, instead of moving onto the right foot at the top of the backswing, has gone onto the left foot. The only way it can move now is

back onto the right side as you hit the ball. Powerless shots result and, from what might be almost a good swing action, true potential is never achieved. It is often caused by trying to keep the head absolutely still throughout the swing.

CURE

Take a golf ball in your hand, and throw it as if it were a pebble you were trying to skim across the water. You will find that your weight moves onto your back foot, and then onto your front foot as you throw the ball.

As this happens your head will move as well. Now throw a second ball, but this time keep your head absolutely still, and the ball will not go as far because your weight does not move sufficiently back and through. This illustrates the stifling effect that a similar movement is having on your swing. You must allow a little head movement to develop in order to transfer the weight onto the right side. Do the turning drill on pages 44–45, feeling how the weight moves from side to side as you turn. It is also good to hit some shots from an uphill lie if possible. In that situation the weight tends to transfer quite readily onto the right foot in the backswing.

FAULT

The spinal angle set at address has been lost and if the ball is to be hit at all this angle must be recreated at impact. Golf is difficult enough without throwing in yet another variable. The player who has this problem usually has trouble turning

and in an effort to swing the arms upwards, the whole spine is raised. You may well be accused of lifting your head, but it is the body that has raised and the head has to go with it!

CURE

To increase suppleness, the turning drill on pages 44–45 should be repeated regularly. When practising, imagine the spine remaining at the same angle, or picture an electric cable just above your head which, if your head touches it, will give you a bad shock. If you swing back correctly you should feel a lot more downward pressure on the right leg and foot.

FAULT

The weight has remained on the right foot as the downswing starts, and consequently the top half of the body has become too active and thrown the clubhead onto an outside path. The ball will be topped, sliced or pulled.

CURE

I want you to imagine (or you can actually do it) that you are going to bounce a tennis ball in front of you, then hit it underarm over the net. As you swing your arm back, your weight will move onto your right foot. Then you will step onto the left foot just before you hit the ball.

This weight transference is what ought to happen in the golf swing, so try to use this picture to cure the fault. As you work on this action, try to keep your head steady and behind the ball until after impact, so that you do not move too laterally towards the target. However, once the ball is struck, let your head move towards the target.

FAULT

The body has not turned through enough, and so the spine is arched backwards. Very often keeping the head down too long will cause this, and it is a movement which will restrict your power and also eventually hurt your neck. You must certainly watch the ball until the clubhead hits it, but overdoing this action is wrong.

CURE

Slowly swing your arms through the impact zone; as they reach the horizontal on the through swing your head should start to rotate towards the target, but try to maintain the spinal angle. Hold that position, then repeat the drill, allowing your arms and body to turn your head. Now extend the follow through so that at the finish the weight is almost fully on the outside of the left foot and your head is facing forwards, is above that foot, and your body is facing just left of the target (see page 43). It may help you to imagine that, as you swing through, someone is standing ahead of you and to your left, and you must finish facing them.

THROUGH THE BAG

When you have learnt the basic golf swing it is simply a matter of tailoring your address position to suit certain clubs and certain shots. I have already stressed that how you stand to the ball encourages or discourages desired movements, and it is only subtle changes to this address position that will make hitting a full wedge shot a slightly different action from hitting a driver.

You can see in this sequence of pictures that the set-up for a short iron, with a fairly narrow stance and the weight favouring the left side will produce a steeper angle of attack on the ball.

SHORT IRONS

For full shots with a sand iron, wedge and 9-iron, whilst the shoulders remain square to the target, the stance, now at its narrowest, should be slightly open. With the weight favouring the left side about 55–60%, your head will be level with, or slightly ahead of the ball. This type of set-up will encourage the steeper swing that is needed for short irons, where accuracy rather than distance is the key. The shoulders will not turn as far as for longer clubs because of the open stance.

Whilst an 8-iron would be described as a short iron, I would recommend that you use the normal mid and long iron set-up with this club, since it is really always used with a full swing.

MIDDLE AND LONG IRONS AND FAIRWAY WOODS

For irons from 1 to 8, and for fairway woods, I would recommend that your stance and body line is square with the weight spread evenly on both feet, and head just behind the ball. The width of stance should increase as the longer clubs are used, but don't overdo it.

As a general guide, your stance with a 5-iron, where the outsides of the feet are just slightly wider than the shoulders, should be the widest you adopt for all irons, as well as for fairway woods. From this set-up, you will readily be able to make a good shoulder turn, the increasing length of shaft of the various clubs progressively making the swing slightly flatter. You do not need to think about this because the set-up will dictate it.

Here, using a wider, squarer stance, and with the weight even, it becomes easier to strike the medium and long irons or fairway woods with maximum power.

DRIVER OR WOOD FROM THE TEE

With the feet and shoulders aligned square to the target the stance is now at its widest, with the outsides of the feet just outside the width of the shoulders.

As you take your address position, when you move your right foot to the right be sure to feel that your head moves in that direction as well, so that about 55–60% of your weight is on the right foot, with the definite feeling of the head being behind the ball.

This set-up will encourage you to take the clubhead away keeping it low to the ground for about the first 18 inches, so that it will return to the ball from a similarly shallow angle of attack.

The fact that the ball is played slightly further forward in the stance than for other shots means that it will be contacted when the clubhead is just starting to ascend.

The 3-wood and driver have the longest shafts, so you will be standing the furthest distance from the ball, which means the plane of the swing will be at its flattest. Do not think about making this happen as your set-up will see to that. Note that because the ball is played further forward, the hands are not as far ahead of the ball as for iron shots.

It is also important to note that as the weight distribution progressively alters from the short iron to the driver, when viewed face-on, the angle of the shoulders is affected. With a short iron they are almost horizontal, but the right shoulder is considerably lower than the left when using a driver.

This set-up, with the weight favouring the right side and the head behind the ball, helps to create the shallow angle of attack needed for the driver or woods from the tee.

HIT IT BETTER

Peter Alliss once said that, 'if you want to hit it further, hit it better'. What sound advice that is, especially for women. We have to face the fact that, apart from a very small percentage of us, we do not have the same power as men. We must, therefore, have good technique with all parts of our body contributing to clubhead speed, applied squarely. For most club golfers this is not an easy task and more often than not they slice shots, thus diminishing power and accuracy. It is true to say that I spend about 90% of my teaching time curing those who slice. Once that is eradicated direction and distance improve. A large part of this chapter is thus devoted to curing the slice.

Those who hook shots are not far from being good golfers and usually a change in set-up will go a long way to curing them.

I have included some advice for those golfers who hit the ball straight, but would like more distance. They may also find the equipment section of this book of interest, because there is no doubt that today's technology can buy you extra yards.

THE SLICE

The problem with this shot, apart from the fact that the ball misses the target, is that it also lacks power. Most ladies would like more power in their swing, so to be hitting the ball in what is a powerless fashion makes no sense. The player who slices hits the ball with an open clubface and this adds loft to the club, so the

The out-to-in swing path can produce three main shapes of shot depending on the position of the clubface at impact.

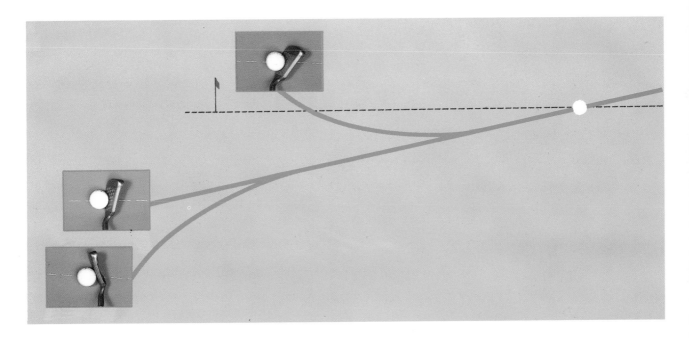

ball not only spins to the right, but also flies much higher than it should, which can lose you valuable distance.

Those who slice also occasionally hit shots that go straight left and so, with what seems like the same swing, they are capable of missing the target either 30 yards right or 30 yards left. They are also very prone to hitting shots off the shank of the club, sending the ball dramatically to the right. Why should they be so versatile, yet so unpredictable? Let's look at the problem in clock face terms, and get a better understanding of what takes place.

The clubhead is swung too much from out-to-in (i.e. too much in the 2 o'clock to 8 o'clock direction).

When the ball slices to the right, the clubface is open to the swing path.

When the ball is pulled to the left, it is square to the swing path.

When the ball starts left then curves to the left, called a pull hook, the clubface is closed to the swing path.

A steep angle of attack with a wood can cause a skied shot.

You can see that the direction of the swing remains constant, but it is the clubface at impact that changes, according to how your hands work through the impact zone.

A further problem presented by this particular swing path is that the club approaches the ball on a steep angle of attack (i.e. too vertically) which directs too much power downwards

A weak grip often results in the clubface being open at impact.

instead of forwards. Deep divots pointing left of the target are often taken. This steep attack also makes it particularly difficult to hit good tee shots.

If you remember, I wrote earlier (page 65) that a shallow angle of attack was needed to hit good tee shots, and the out-to-in path, when severe, does not provide the correct angle of attack. The ball is often struck with the top edge of the face of the wood, leaving tell-tale scuff marks and resulting in a skied shot.

That is what happens to the clubhead, but what causes this to happen?

Firstly, many golfers grip the club in such a manner that they cannot return the clubface squarely to the ball. The hands are usually positioned wrongly and the grip pressure is too tight. These factors combine to leave the club face open at impact.

Even those golfers whose grip is correct may find the correct hand action unnatural, or fail to understand how their hands and arms should work in the swing, thus failing to square the clubface at impact.

For many players, setting up squarely to the ball is one of the most difficult problems, and most stand with the shoulders hips, knees and

An open set-up will cause an out-to-in swing.

Even from a good back-swing the club can be cast onto an outside path.

feet open. This alone will cause the clubface to cut across the ball at impact, thus imparting slice spin causing the ball to veer to the right.

Even if the address position is correct many golfers have great difficulty swinging the club head back to the ball on an inside path.

Whilst the top of the backswing position may be fine, the right shoulder and arm, which may feel the strongest source of power at this point, become too active too soon, and the clubhead is thrown onto an outside path. This action also causes a shank.

Let's see if we can cure, or at least reduce the slice. In all honesty, if you have sliced the ball for several years, it will take some time (months, not days) to completely eradicate it. But don't worry, you do not have to hit the ball perfectly straight to score well, but if you can narrow the sector into which you are likely to hit it, as well as gain some length, then your scores should tumble.

GRIP AND ADDRESS

The first things to check are your grip and set-up (refer back to pages 14–31). It is likely that your grip has been weak in one or both hands, so make sure that you can see two to two-and-a-half knuckles on the left hand and that both 'V's formed by the thumbs and forefingers point between the right eye and right shoulder. Do not grip too tightly.

Check your alignment and ball position. Do this by laying a club down across your feet, then ask someone to hold a club across the front of your shoulders. It is almost certain that your feet, hips and shoulders have been open, and this way you can confirm it. They should aim parallel to the target line.

You have possibly had the ball a little too far forward, encouraging the shoulders to open, so check this facing a mirror.

Believe me, if you have been standing with your shoulders open, they will feel as if they are aiming a long way right when you stand with them parallel to the target line.

THE HAND ACTION

Once your set-up is correct the swing needs changing. First let's look at the hand and arm action. Many golfers have the wrong picture of what they are trying to do. It is the action of the clubhead descending onto the ball that gets it airborne, but often a player will try to scoop the ball into the air, which unfortunately opens the clubface.

You may in fact have almost the correct hand action, but it may be rather sluggish, but by practising a simple drill you can improve it quite quickly.

Stand with your feet quite close together and grip down the shaft a little with a 7-iron. Swing your arms back until the left arm is horizontal, the wrists fully cocked so that the shaft is at 90° to the left forearm. Now swing the clubhead through to a similar position, so that your right arm is about horizontal, the wrists fully cocked, and the shaft at 90° to the right arm.

At first this can be done without a ball, just trying to create as much of a swishing action as you can with your hands and forearms.

The hands do not rotate in quite such an exaggerated way in the full swing, but for those whose hand action has been non-existent or too slow, this is a marvellous drill.

If the right hand works incorrectly under the left hand, it tends to open the clubface at impact.

This swishing drill helps to create the correct hand action where the right hand and arm rotate correctly over the left through impact.

One other way to appreciate how and when the hands work is to hold the club in your right hand on the shaft near the head, as if it were a stick. Imagine you are going to hit a daisy and · you will find that your arm swings down and your hand swishes the shaft. Do this several times, then hold the club correctly in both hands, and repeat the action. This will give you a good impression of how your hands should work.

It would also be useful to reread pages 48–49, which deal with hand action.

Hold the club shaft as shown here, just in one hand and pretend you are trying to hit a daisy. It will help you create the correct hand action.

THE SWING PATH

This can be one of the most difficult parts of the golf swing to alter, but there are several ways to encourage the correct actions to take place.

First, place two clubs down parallel to your target line, then angle the one outside the ball so that it aims to the right of the target, in the 3.30–9.30 position in clock face terms.

When you swing try to make the clubhead swing parallel to this outer club both on the backswing, and most importantly on the downswing. Do this without a ball at first, and you will feel that you are swinging much more to the right of your target than is usual. This is the correct feeling to cultivate.

Angle the outside club towards 9.30 on an imaginary clock face and it will encourage the correct inside swing path.

One of the best exercises that I know, which not only develops the correct swing path but also good hand action, is to stand with a narrow stance and the right foot back from the target line. From this position it is easy to swing the club on the inside, and because the body cannot move out of the way through impact, the hands tend to rotate naturally.

Many people I have taught have hit the ball so well like this that they would like to use it on the golf course. There is nothing wrong with it and even if you do not play like this, a few practice swings in this fashion on the way round would always help.

Many golfers have played tennis, so let me give you a tennis analogy. If you have a racquet then try this. If you were to hit a forehand topspin shot down the right hand tramlines, you would have to do this with your right arm and the racquet starting close into your right side, then swinging away from your body as you hit the ball. The hand and arm would rotate anti-clockwise, so that the racquet head is facing almost square to the horizontal at the end of the stroke. This is very similar to what you need to feel in your swing.

With the right foot withdrawn back behind the left, the club readily approaches the ball from the inside.

Imagine hitting a topspin forehand into the right tramlines to create the inside attack.

For those of you who may be left handed, but play golf right handed, imagine you are hitting a backhand top spin into the right hand tramlines. In this instance your back would start half turned to the net, and your arm and hand would have to rotate through impact, with the left elbow folding. In both cases the racquet head is swung from inside the target line, just as we want the clubhead to be.

This drill is best practised where you can see yourself, with a mirror or window to your right. Make your backswing, then look to your right and, keeping your head in that position, start your downswing, stopping your hands at waist height.

You will find that, almost without exception, you will swing your arms and the club on the inside. It is quite difficult to throw the club onto an outside path from this position.

Swing it back to the top and repeat this movement several times without stopping, all the while keeping your head turned to the right. As your arms swing down your hips should turn back to an almost square position and some weight should transfer onto your left foot. Once you can do this quite easily, focus on a spot where the ball might be, trying to reproduce the same action. The beauty of this drill is that you can do it indoors.

If you are left handed, but play golf right handed, imagine hitting a topspin backhand to the right tramlines to create the inside attack.

At the top of your backswing look to your right and begin the downswing. You will readily swing down on the correct path.

For the slightly more experienced golfer, or someone really trying to draw shots, put an umbrella in the ground about four feet ahead of the ball on the target line, then try to start the ball to the right of the umbrella. To do this you must attack the ball from the inside.

A more experienced player could address the ball out of the heel of the club, but then hit it out of the middle. This will force the club to attack from the inside.

For the better player, address the ball out of the heel of the club, then try to hit it out of the middle. You have to re-route the club on a more inward path on the downswing, thus creating more of a draw shot.

Different drills work for different players, so find out which of these help you most. If you can cure your slice you will definitely hit the ball straighter and further.

THE HOOK

This type of shot, where the ball usually starts right of the target and then veers dramatically to the left, tends to be the better player's weakness. They will have developed quite strong hand action which closes the clubface at impact, and perhaps have not adjusted their grip according to their strength and ability.

Distance is not usually a problem, but the direction can be, as a ball with this type of spin tends to run a long way on landing. Because a closed clubface reduces the loft, the ball will fly lower than usual.

The player who hooks the ball often hits shots which go straight right. Let's look at this problem in clock face terms and see what needs to be corrected.

Because the ball curves too much to the left, to offset this the clubhead is swung too much from inside the line, from the 4 to 10 o'clock direction.

When the ball curves to the left, the clubface is closed to the swing path.

The in-to-out swing path can produce three main shapes of shot depending on the position of the clubface at impact.

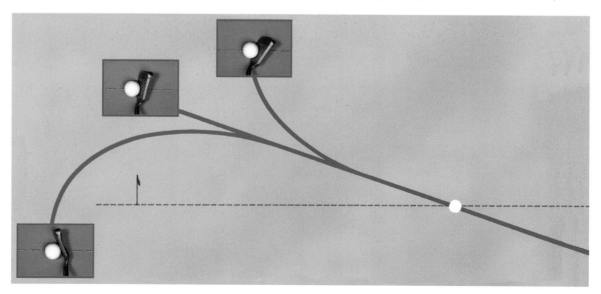

When the ball goes straight right, called a push, the clubface is square to the swing path.

When the ball starts right then curves right, called a push-slice, the clubface is open to the swing path.

The swing path remains constant while the clubface at impact varies according to the exact hand action.

The exaggerated inside path also affects the angle of attack, making it too shallow for crisp iron shots, although shots from good lies, and from tee pegs would not suffer too much.

The player who swings in this fashion is not too far from getting it right. It is just that the good features have been exaggerated.

If you can hit the ball while the clubhead is still travelling from just inside the target line, and have the clubface square to the target, then you will hit a draw, which is perhaps the most desirable shot of all. It will start just to the right of the target then curve back towards it, and will be a powerful shot. How, then, can we turn a hook into a draw?

The exaggerated inside path creates a shallow angle of attack which can cause topped shots.

Left: A strong grip will almost always cause a hook.

Below: Check your alignment as well; standing closed to the target creates an in-to-out swing path.

GRIP AND ADDRESS

It is quite possible that your grip is strong, but because you use your hands very well, you need a more neutral grip, with perhaps only two left hand knuckles showing, and both 'V's aimed more towards the right eye. You may need to experiment to find the exact grip that allows you to hit the ball hard but does not close the clubface.

Your feet and shoulders have probably been closed, so check this by placing a club across your feet and have someone place one across the front of your shoulders. Also check that the ball is not too far back in your stance. Pages 14–31 will help you with this.

THE SWING

The alterations to your set-up should take care of the major corrections needed, but it will help you to groove the correct swing path if you practise with a club on the ground outside the ball, parallel to the target line. As the clubhead swings back, it should make just a gently curving inward arc, and you should feel as though you swing it back towards 3 o'clock for longer than usual. Try to picture it returning along a similar path, so that the clubhead will be approaching the ball more from the 3.30 than 4 o'clock direction.

Below: As Marie-Laure de Lorenzi swings through the ball her left hip is turning out of the way, which helps her to keep the clubface square at impact.

Get your set-up correct on the practice ground, using clubs on the ground to help you align straight.

Be sure that you swing through the ball so that you finish with your body facing just left of target. By doing this your legs should now be working correctly and your hips should then be opening as your arms swing through impact. This will prevent the clubface from closing too quickly and will make straighter shots more likely.

Better players may also need to feel that the left wrist remains firmer through impact, so that the hands and forearms do not rotate so quickly.

DAMAGE LIMITATION

All golfers would accept that golf is a difficult and demanding game, yet our choice of club can either minimize our faults, or make them worse.

When the straighter faced clubs, such as the driver, 1, 2, 3, and 4-irons are used, the ball is contacted nearer its equator and consequently maximum sidespin is imparted. When the more lofted clubs are used more backspin is imparted and this, to some extent, will enable you to hit the ball straighter.

This explains why the player who slices the long irons will pull the short iron shots. In each case the clubhead is travelling in the same direction, i.e. out-to-in, but the short irons will create more backspin and little of the sidespin that causes the ball to curve off-line, so the direction of the swing path will be the direction of the ball.

It would therefore make sense that the straight faced clubs are not used if you either slice or hook the ball violently. Most golfers would lower their scores, not by hitting the ball further, but by hitting it straighter, so try to eliminate your faults but help yourself by teeing off with a 3, 4 or 5-wood, and using the more lofted irons.

Even those players who hit the ball quite straight can enhance their chances of hitting the ball well by their choice of club. Generally speaking ladies are not very adept at hitting long irons, (i.e. 1 to 4). These have little loft, which means (a) they must be struck very accurately and, (b) because they lack loft, they need to be struck quite firmly to create enough backspin to get the ball airborne.

Whilst this problem is offset slightly when the ball is hit from a tee, with a less than perfect lie on the fairway lack of clubhead speed through lack of strength could cause problems.

This is why ladies are often much better fairway wood players, because the extra weight in the head and the additional loft make them easier to hit. I know several single figure players who now carry a 7-wood, which is roughly the

Above: With the straighter faced clubs the ball is struck nearer its equator, but is struck lower down with the more lofted clubs.

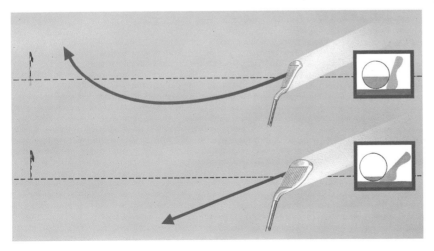

Left: With the out-to-in swing path the long irons slice and the short irons are pulled left.

equivalent of a 3- or 4-iron. Indeed, Lotte Neumann, the Swedish professional who won the American Open Championship in 1988, now carries a 7-wood and leaves the 3-iron out of her bag. If you cannot hit the longer irons very well, do not despair, but make good use of the fairway woods.

You may therefore ask, what is the secret of hitting a fairway wood? There really is no secret, but if you set up correctly picture sweeping the ball from the grass rather than hitting down on the ball.

In fact many ladies have great difficulty trying to hit down, and instead tend to sweep all shots, and this is why they can play their fairway woods quite well. For those who do not hit the woods well, if you concentrate on keeping the clubhead low to the ground on the backswing until it has passed your right foot, this will encourage the correct shallow contact.

At the start of the backswing with fairway woods, keep the clubhead low to the ground to encourage a sweeping action through the ball.

THE TEE SHOT

I wrote in an earlier chapter that for all long shots we learn a golf swing, then tailor our address position to suit the club we are using. This was never truer than when hitting a tee shot, and it is worth looking at this in a little more detail.

First of all your choice of club is critical. Because the shot is called a drive, do not fall into the trap of thinking that unless you use the driver you are not playing the game as it should be played.

In fact, as a general rule I reckon that if your handicap is above 18 you should not use the driver, but take a 3, 4, or even a 5-wood from the tee. Your task is to hit the ball down the **fairway** as far as you can, not to hit it out of sight into the trees or deep rough.

The more lofted woods make the task easier. For players with a handicap below 18, then by all means consider using a driver, but check the loft before you buy one. Drivers vary in loft from about 8° to 13°, and so vary in difficulty of use. Check yours, and if you have problems hitting it, and it does not have 11° or more of loft, then I would suggest you might buy another, or use your 3-wood.

How and where you tee the ball will either help or hinder you. As a guide for the height of the tee, the general rule is that half the ball should be above the top of the clubface.

Therefore, depending on the depth of the face this height will vary. When you tee the ball, choose a spot on the tee that offers a smooth and firm area both for your feet and the club's path. Remember that you can legally tee up in the area that is between the tee boxes, extending backwards two club lengths, so make full use of it.

If there is trouble on the right, tee up on that side and, conversely, if there is any trouble on the left, tee up that side and you will find it easier to play away from any potential danger.

With regard to the swing itself, the only real danger is that you do not let your shoulders become open because the ball is played further forward in the stance than for an iron shot.

To get its maximum power the clubhead must attack the ball from an inside path, and this will be virtually impossible from an open shouldered set-up.

It would be a good idea to ask your playing partner to check your shoulder alignment from time to time, but only during a friendly round, not in competition, as that would be against the rules.

Always try to maintain good rhythm with your tee shots. It is very tempting to try to hit the ball harder than usual, but keep the same pace and tempo that you would use for say, a 5-iron, and your results should improve.

Keep your head behind the ball until it is struck so that you have the feeling of hitting the ball away from you, but be sure to swing through to a balanced finish, with your head above your left foot and weight on that side.

Short in height but not in length on the golf course, 1987 British Open champion Alison Nicholas swings to a balanced finish, weight on her left side, right heel released from the ground.

The various lofts of a driver, 3-wood and 5-wood. Driver lofts do vary but you should never buy one with less than 10° loft.

5 WOOD

3 WOOD

DRIVER

HITTING IT FURTHER

Once you have good technique, where all parts of the body are contributing to clubhead speed, squarely applied, how can you improve your distance?

You have to make the clubhead swing faster, but not at the expense of accuracy or else that speed is wasted. In trying to create more speed all parts of the system must be upgraded.

For instance, there is no point in trying to make your arms swing faster if your hips and shoulders do not similarly move more quickly; and there is no point is using a faster hand action if this closes the face of the club too quickly.

As you play more golf, you will become stronger, and the exercises at the back of this book will help you with this, but perhaps one or two aspects of the swing are worth looking at a little more closely.

Above right: From a square set-up, long-hitting Corinne Dibnah, the 1988 British Open champion, takes the clubhead away low on an inside path, a positive move for maximum distance.

Right: Laura Davies keeps her head well behind the ball as she powerfully drives the clubhead towards the target.

To find out your natural speed of swing, set up without a club with your palms about two inches apart. Now make your swing and you will find that you move your entire body in a smooth manner.

What will happen is that your elbows and hips will move in tandem back and through; so the top half of your body and the bottom half are synchronized at the correct pace for you.

Repeat this exercise about five to ten times, then hit shots and you will find that you will swing in a relaxed effortless manner at your ideal pace. The ball will go further and straighter with seemingly less effort.

The backswing should create the power in the swing and as you become stronger and more flexible you can create more torque in the swing.

This means you will get a greater sensation of the top half of your body winding up like a spring against the resistance of the lower half. In order to create this you may need to adjust the angle of your feet at address so that the right foot is not turned out so much, but be sure that this does not prevent you from making a full turn.

Alternatively, if you have been raising the left heel, keep it flat on the ground, or closer to the ground and you will create a stronger turn.

A serious word of warning, the above advice is only for those with no back or neck problems, and not for those whose suppleness is waning!

It is very easy to think that the faster and the further you swing the club back, the further you will hit the ball. Some of the top women professionals do swing the club past the horizontal at the top of the backswing, but they have superb club control, and are able to get maximum clubhead speed at impact. Sadly this is not always true for the amateur golfer, accuracy is sometimes lost, and maximum club-head speed does not coincide with impact.

Let me give you an analogy. If I was asked to jump forwards ten feet from a standing position, I could not do it. If I was allowed a run up of say, 30 yards, I could make a good attempt at the jump. If I was given a run up of 100 yards, I would not be able to maintain full speed by the time I reached the take-off point and would be slowing down. This is what can happen if the backswing is too long; the wrists tend to uncock too soon and so maximum speed is reached before impact. Experiment and see if a slightly

shorter backswing helps you to accelerate through impact rather than decelerate.

Do not become ball bound. Many golfers think the swing ends with hitting the ball. It doesn't. You are trying to swing the club in a circle about the fixed point at the top of your spine. Hit through the ball and finish facing the target. You'll be surprised how much distance you can gain by this one swing thought.

For those who are not so supple and for whom making a shoulder turn is rather difficult, you must work on good hand and arm action.

Refer back to pages 67–73 on hand action and curing a slice and practise the drills in those sections. It may be an advantage for you to set up with your feet and shoulders **slightly** closed, which will help you to get the inside attack that is essential for maximum distance. Try to swing your arms and make your hands swish the club, that is the secret for you.

Once you have learned to use all parts of your body correctly then you should be able to draw the ball, i.e. put spin on it that makes it curve from right to left, which is the strongest flight for a woman golfer to use. You should experiment by positioning the ball back a **little** in the stance and making sure that as the club approaches from the inside path, the right hand and arm hit the ball firmly, rotating over the

The superb swing of hard-hitting Corinne Dibnah shows she attacks from the inside, with the right hand and arm rotating over the left through impact, producing a long draw.

left through the impact zone. This action must be timed correctly, and you will need to practise to see if a **slightly** stronger grip helps to this end, or whether an adjustment in shoulder alignment helps you to start the ball just right of the target. But do try to keep to your natural rhythm, don't just thrash at the ball, because you will not hit it **consistently** better that way.

It is worth experimenting with equipment, because men's clubs may help you to hit the ball further once you are strong enough to use them. There is more detailed information about equipment on pages 152–157, but, providing by the end of the round you can still swing them under control, you could easily hit the ball five to ten yards further with the **correct** men's clubs for you.

Not all professionals are totally orthodox, yet they still play well because they swing the clubhead towards the target and have the clubface square at impact.

Dottie Mochrie has a very upright backswing but it has not prevented her from becoming very successful despite the fact that it is not how most teachers would encourage their pupils to swing.

A look at a few other players will emphasize that not all their swings are orthodox.

Helen Alfredsson

At the top of Swedish golfer Helen Alfredsson's swing (below) her club shaft aims a long way right of target, but in her case it is because she is so supple that she turns her shoulders through more than 90°.

Had Helen's shaft aimed right because she had swung the club too much to the inside, more towards 4 o'clock on the backswing, she would not have achieved this superb position just prior to impact where the shaft is parallel to the target line when it is horizontal.

USA Solheim Cup player Dottie Mochrie maintains control and consistency even from this very long and upright backswing. It works for her but the club golfer would struggle to achieve their best from this position.

Lotte Neumann

Another great player from Sweden, Lotte Neumann won the American Open in 1988, and has competed very successfully on both sides of the Atlantic for several years. She is very consistent, and no wonder, because her swing is so controlled, yet powerful.

Whilst Dottie Mochrie swings the club past the horizontal, Lotte has more of a three-quarter swing, where the shaft, certainly on her iron shots, does not even reach the horizontal. Notice that her left heel is still on the ground, and compare this to Mochrie's.

By keeping her left heel down she creates a good coiling action where her body turns against the resistance of her legs. She then makes a strong move with her legs and hips on the downswing, before releasing her power through good hand action.

You will see how firm the back of her left wrist is at impact, as her right hand strikes against it.

Despite the good use of her legs her head is still in its address position. Some club golfers making a similar movement can tend to move too laterally towards the target and thus lose power.

She also holds her spinal angle very well, looking at the turf until the ball is well on its way. Whilst many golfers would not hit their maximum distance from Lotte's backswing position, she remains powerful because the attack is from the inside, and is well timed. The danger for most players from this backswing would be to use the top half of the body too early, either casting the club with their hands onto an outside path, or else turning the body open to the target too soon. Whenever the clubhead approaches the ball from the outside, you are liable to lose power as well as accuracy.

One could not really call Lotte's swing unorthodox, but more compact than some. Technically it is superb and her rhythm and timing allow her to make the most of her talents. Whilst it is the swing of a young, fit person, she is always a good player to watch, because her swing is simple and unhurried.

Laura Davies

Laura Davies, a former British and American Open champion, is currently the most exciting player in the world to watch, yet her swing, based on natural ability rather than structured lessons, has its idiosyncrasies. She addresses the ball with her shoulders open and employs a strong left hand grip, which would make some players hook the ball, but her set-up face-on for a driver shows her weight correctly favouring the right side, head nicely behind the ball.

She makes a powerful turn in the backswing, but at the start of her downswing her left heel does not retun to its original position but seems to swivel towards the target, which probably makes it more difficult for Laura to clear her hips.

Despite her departures from the norm, at impact she attacks the ball from the inside and her hands are returning to their address position, so the clubface will be square at impact. Both heels leave the ground as she makes her powerful strike.

Her finish, though, is classic and, despite being one of the hardest hitters of a golf ball, her balance is maintained beautifully on the left side, her body having turned through well left of the target.

She hits the ball consistently well and it is only when she gets a little open at address that she is not at her best.

Patty Sheehan

LPGA Hall of Fame member and 1992
American and British Open champion Patty
Sheehan to my mind has a superb swing worth
watching and copying. An orthodox set-up
leads to a superb backswing and we can see
that, just prior to impact, she has retained a
great deal of her wrist-cock until late in
the downswing.

As she then releases the power of her hands
into the shot, her right knee moves towards the
target and her hips clear so that she finishes
beautifully balanced on her left side, with her
body turned to face the target.

Sadly, still photographs do not adequately
convey the superb rhythm and minimum effort
she seems to use. Watch her if you can.

TROUBLE SHOTS

It is only on a driving range or for a tee shot that you have the chance to hit the ball from a guaranteed flat and even lie. For the rest of the shots from the fairway and rough you will encounter many different types of lie, each requiring some sort of adjustment to the usual stance or swing. This is what makes golf so interesting and challenging as no two rounds ever present exactly the same problems. Learning to play from a variety of lies only comes with experience.

If, for example, your course is fairly flat you will have some difficulty coping with a hilly course the first time you play it. Your course may have little rough, but you can rest assured that at some time in your golfing life you will be playing from the rough and so need to know the best way to tackle these shots.

Windy links courses often call for you to hit the ball high or low at specific times if you are to get the best from your round; so the variety of shots in your repertoire grows the longer you play. Most of the adjustments need to be made at address, and these changes will affect your swing accordingly.

SLOPING LIES

These shots fall into two main categories:

(a) uphill and downhill lies, and
(b) sidehill lies where the ball is above or below your feet.

Think of them as two different families of shots and you will find it easier to remember what adjustments have to be made.

UPHILL LIES

When you play from a level lie, your spine is at right angles to the ground, and this is what you must try to achieve when you play a long shot from an uphill lie.

Put more weight on your **right** foot and angle your spine so that your right shoulder will feel lower than normal. This set-up will increase the loft on your club, so that a 6-iron may have the loft of a 7- or 8-iron, depending on the severity of the slope.

Consequently, the ball will fly higher, so to achieve a 6-iron distance you must use a straighter faced club, perhaps a 5- or 4-iron. Play the ball further forward in your stance, nearer your **left** foot, as this will encourage you to sweep the ball away.

When playing uphill put more weight on your right foot and play the ball forward in your stance.

As you swing, try to make the clubhead follow the contours of the ground, so that you will get the feeling of almost hitting up on the ball.

It is difficult to transfer the weight onto the left side through impact, and therefore the hands tends to become more active, closing the clubface. The ball is likely to finish a little left of target, so aim a little right to allow for this.

If you have an uphill lie around the green, it is better to put your weight on the **left** foot with the spine more at right angles to the horizontal, feeling that you lean into the slope.

This will ensure a downward strike, with the clubhead coming to quite an abrupt halt. Providing the slope is gentle, lower handicap players might be able to play set-up as for the long shots, which will give higher softer shots.

DOWNHILL LIES

These are more difficult to play than uphill shots, and are shots you really should practise if possible. The adjustments are the opposite to the uphill lie, so if you can remember how to play that, then just do the opposite for this shot. But let's look at it in detail.

The spine must be at right angles to the slope, so put more weight on the **left** foot, and feel that your left shoulder is lower than usual. You must also put your head more above your left foot than the right. This set-up will reduce the loft on the club, so a 6-iron could be more like a 5- or 4-iron depending on the slope, therefore to hit the ball 6-iron distance a more lofted club, perhaps a 7 or 8, is used. To ensure good contact the ball is played back in the stance nearer the **right** foot.

On the backswing you must swing the arms more upward than usual with little conscious body turn, using an early wrist cock on severe slopes in order to avoid hitting the ground

For a downhill shot put more weight on your left foot and play the ball back in your stance.

If you have an uphill lie around the green put more weight on your left foot so that you lean into the slope.

Sweep the ball away, driving the club down the slope. When you are near the green with a downhill shot, have your weight more on your right foot.

behind the ball. Most importantly you must be certain to swing the clubhead down the slope as you swing through, avoiding any tendency to lean back onto the right foot to try to hit the ball up into the air. Trust the loft on the club, and drive the clubhead down the slope. You may even fall off balance on severe slopes but as long as you are balanced at impact this is quite acceptable. The ball may fade or be pushed to the right so aim left and allow for this.

On downhill shots around the green use the same set-up, but you could well encounter a severe slope where it is impossible to keep your balance standing this way. In this instance put your weight on the **right** foot with the spine vertical, and the ball back in your stance. In very extreme circumstances the ball may even be outside your right foot, and you will have to grip down on the metal shaft of the club. The shot is played using the hands and arms with little body movement.

For the uphill and downhill shots from the fairway remember that the weight is on the low foot (**l**o**w** and **w**eight both have a **W**), and the ball is by the high foot.

BALL BELOW FEET

Whilst it is the weight that is altered for uphill and downhill lies, it is the posture that changes for sidehill lies. When the ball is below the feet you must angle forward more from the hips, and increase the knee flex in order to get the clubhead down to the level of the ball. You will find that your weight wants to tip towards your toes, but you must keep the weight on the balls of your feet and also have sufficient weight on your heels to maintain good balance throughout. Position the ball just slightly more forward than usual.

This set-up makes it difficult to turn the body, so it is mainly the arms and hands that make the swing. Because of lack of body turn, the swing path tends to be steep and from out-to-in, resulting in shots that slice, so aim left to allow for this.

If the weight falls forward during the swing, it is easy to shank these shots, i.e. the ball is struck with the shank of the club and shoots violently right. To offset this tendency, address the ball at the middle to toe end of the clubface, and swing easily, concentrating on your balance. Avoid using straight faced clubs, and in severe circumstances be content to keep the ball in play. This is one of the most disliked shots in golf, and one of the most difficult. Never try to hit the ball too hard, but focus on keeping your balance.

Shots around the green are played in the same way.

With the ball below your feet you need to get closer to the ball, but maintain your balance carefully. Never be tempted into over-swinging on this shot.

BALL ABOVE FEET

When the ball is above the feet do not angle forward so much from the hips, so the spine stays more upright than from level lies. With slightly more weight on the heels than normal, play the ball more centrally, and grip down the club a little.

This set-up tends to flatten the swing and gives the feeling of swinging more around the body. The result is that the ball is likely to draw, so aim to the right to allow for it. From a gentle slope it is quite possible to use a fairway wood if distance is needed. Beginners can often hit good shots from this lie, as it encourages the body to turn correctly.

Shots around the green, using short irons are played in the same way, and in some instances, where the ball is very much above the feet, you may have to grip down on the club almost to the metal shaft, in order to be able to play the shot.

With all four sloping lies, the swing will feel different than normal, so have a practice swing before you hit the ball to familiarise yourself with how the swing will feel, and do not hit the ball too hard. The only exception to this is if the ball is only just above the feet when a full swing can be made easily.

Right: With the ball above your feet you stand a little further from the ball so you need to stand a little taller. As the ball is likely to draw from this position aim more to the right.

SHAPING YOUR SHOTS

The better golfer you become, the easier it is to shape your shots and the more adventurous you can become. It is the address position that makes it a simple task to hit the ball as desired. After that, as usual, a little practice will work wonders.

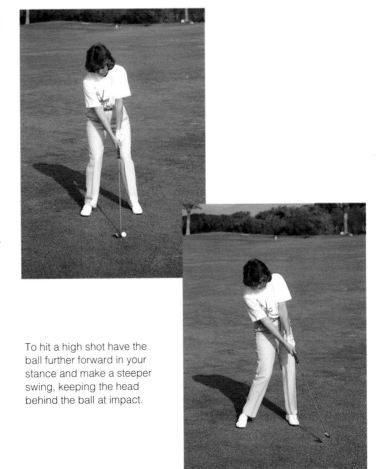

HIGH SHOTS

These are best attempted only from a good lie where there is a cushion of grass beneath the ball. Obviously the lofted clubs will naturally hit the ball high, but you may need to play over trees or to an elevated green, and need height as well as length, in which case you would hit a medium iron.

Play the ball further forward in your stance, with a little more weight on your right side, the right knee slightly more flexed than usual. The shaft should not slope so much towards your target, but be in a more vertical position (in golfing terms called laid back), which results in the clubface being more lofted. Your head should have the definite feeling of being behind the ball.

Try to make your arm swing steeper, with a little more wrist and hand action, but do not let the right hand cross over the left through impact as this would deloft the clubface. Instead make it work under the left hand, keeping your head behind the ball.

Playing high shots this way the blade will remain square to the target, but in extreme circumstances, especially from bad lies, you could open the clubface, and aim left of the target, to produce a high slicing type of shot.

To hit a high shot have the ball further forward in your stance and make a steeper swing, keeping the head behind the ball at impact.

LOW SHOTS

These are especially useful on windy days, or if you are playing from under trees. The lower numbered clubs naturally hit the ball lower because they have little loft, but there will be some occasions when you need to hit the ball extremely low.

Play the ball back of centre in your stance, slightly closing your shoulders, but keeping your hands forward so that the shaft slopes considerably towards the target, but the blade remains square. This set-up will naturally deloft the clubface (called hooding in golfing terms), so could make a 4-iron more like a 1-iron depending how far back the ball is played.

If you are playing the ball under low branches and must keep it only a few inches off the ground, then you would possibly position the ball level with, or even outside your right foot.

Favour the weight on the left foot, grip down the shaft and make a firm wristed swing. Even for full length shots the follow through should be curtailed so that the swing is more punchy.

This set-up and swing may produce a draw shot, where the ball starts right of target, then curves back towards it. Never hit the ball hard if you are playing shots into the wind, because this will only create more backspin which sends the ball higher. It is far better to take two clubs more than usual, grip down and swing easy.

Whilst the high shot ideally needs a decent lie, the low shot can be played from almost any lie you might encounter on the course, and can safely be attempted by almost all categories of player.

To keep the ball low, maybe to stay under overhanging branches, play it further back in your stance and make a punchy firm-wristed swing.

PLAYING FROM ROUGH

Whilst the technique of playing from rough contributes greatly to the success of the shot, there is no doubt about the fact that the strength of the player does have a great influence on the outcome. Men have more strength and therefore usually escape successfully from the less hospitable parts of the course. Perhaps one could argue that they also get more practice at playing these shots!

But ladies, do not despair, there are simple ways of playing these shots proficiently which even the inexperienced player can adopt.

Your first important decision is the choice of club, and this is governed mainly by the lie.

If the ball is lying in light rough, depending on the length of shot required, you could use any club from a sand iron to a 5-iron, or maybe a 5- or 7-wood.

If the ball is in deep rough, getting the ball back onto the fairway is the main objective rather than going for distance. A sand iron, with its heavy clubhead, is usually the best choice.

The clubs to avoid in either situation are the long irons, or a 3-wood.

The two main methods of playing from rough, are to hit the ball out low so that it will run, or to hit it out higher with less run.

You must make your choice depending on the situation, and in Chapter 8 of this book, I have given some guidelines which will be helpful.

If you choose the lower running shot, play the ball back in your stance, hands ahead of the ball, weight on the left foot. Make a steep backswing and concentrate on hitting down on the ball; the follow through may well be curtailed depending on the thickness of the rough.

Because there is grass behind the ball the steep swing is necessary so that the clubhead does not get caught up either on the backswing or downswing. This grass also prevents backspin being applied, so the ball will run on landing.

If you need to hit the ball higher, or are in very deep rough, set up with your shoulders, hips, knees and feet open, ball central, and weight favouring the left foot. Use a lofted club, but open the face slightly. This set up will encourage a steep out-to-in swing that will hit the ball high. Because of the grass around the ball backspin is impossible, so allow for the ball to run a little on landing.

In each of these methods have a practice swing, so that you can feel how much the grass will affect the clubhead through impact. This is one of the few instances when a firmer grip than usual, especially with the left hand, is needed. Also grip down on the club as that will always give you more control.

From the rough never be over-ambitious. The priority is to get the ball back on the fairway at the first attempt. A 5- or 7-wood can be used from light rough, but favour a lofted iron from deep rough.

PLAYING FROM DIVOTS

Sadly the ball will not always be in a good lie and will sometimes come to rest in a divot, from which you cannot expect to play the ball in your normal fashion. You must use the same set-up and swing as when playing the lower shot out of the rough, punching the ball out.

This will enable the club to descend steeply on the ball, and it will come out low and run. If the ball sits at the front of the divot, do not play it so far back in the stance, but use the same type of punchy swing. The one problem with this situation is that the ball may be deflected by the edge of the divot, so do not be too ambitious.

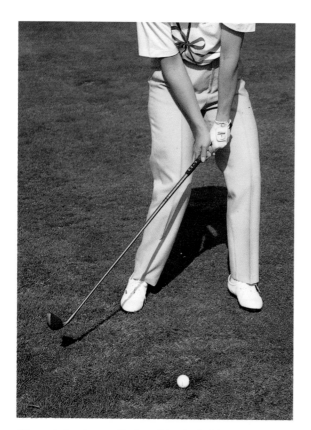

When playing from a divot, position the ball back in your stance with your weight on your left side and swing steeply.

CURVING YOUR SHOTS

You may sometimes find that an obstruction, such as a tree, intervenes between the ball and the target. You will generally have two main choices; hit the ball sideways or curve it around the obstruction.

It is usually better for the higher handicap player to take the first option, but as you improve you will be more capable of shaping shots to order. Having said that, you really must practise these shots before attempting them on the course or in competition. It is not particularly difficult for a good player to move the ball in either direction, but the amount of curve is more difficult to judge.

THE INTENTIONAL FADE

Choice of club is important, because it is much easier to fade or slice the longer, straighter faced irons. If you do not need to hit the ball very far, grip down on perhaps a 5-iron, rather than trying to use a 7-iron. If you need maximum distance a 3-wood, or for the better player even a driver in the right circumstances would be acceptable.

Set up with the clubface aimed at the target, with the ball forward in your stance and your feet and shoulders aimed left, approximately parallel to the direction in which you want the ball to start.

Your hands will be in a weaker position than usual on the grip, and from this set-up you will be able to swing the club on a steep, out-to-in path with an open clubface.

The ball should readily produce a fade that curves from left to right, but if your natural shot is a draw, you may need to make a more upright arm swing and keep the back of the left hand firmer through impact to prevent any anti-clockwise rotation of the hands which would close the clubface.

If you increase the amount you aim to the left, the fade can become a slice.

Remember that a sliced shot will fly higher and go a shorter distance than usual with the club being used. If there is a lot of grass between the clubface and the ball at impact you will not be able to impart much sidespin on the ball, so it may just go in the direction that the swing is aimed, which is your shoulder line, not the line from the ball to the target.

To fade the ball stand open to the target but aim the clubface where you want the ball to finish.

THE INTENTIONAL DRAW

When you hit a draw shot the clubface is closed to the swing path at impact and has a reduced amount of loft. For this reason, if you try to draw the long irons, you may find the ball difficult to control. By closing the face you may be turning a 3-iron into a 1- or 2-iron, so consider this before you choose your club.

Set up with the clubface aimed at the target, the ball back in the stance, with your feet and shoulders aimed right of the target, approximately parallel to the direction in which you want the ball to start.

Your hands will be in a stronger position than usual on the grip, and from this set-up you will be able to make an in-to-out swing with the clubface closed to the swing path. This should create a draw shot that curves from right to left. If your natural shot is a fade or slice, you may need to swing your arms a little flatter, make a bigger shoulder turn in the backswing, then try to make the right hand and arm rotate over the left through impact. Keep the grip light.

If you aim further to the right, the draw can become a hook shot.

If you hit a draw or hook, the ball will fly lower and run further than usual for the club that you are using. If grass intervenes between the clubface and the ball, then you will not be able to impart much sidespin, and the ball may simply fly in the direction the swing is aimed, i.e. parallel to your shoulders.

With both the intentional fade and draw, always be certain to aim so that there is no possibility of hitting the tree or obstruction that may be ahead of you.

If you are playing into the wind, the curve will be accentuated; if you are playing down wind, the curve will be straightened out to some degree. If there is a cross wind, it will either exaggerate or lessen the curve depending on the shot and the direction of the wind.

This chapter has covered most of the difficult shots that you will face during a round, but I do stress that it is only by experience that you will know automatically how to adapt to play these shots from the lies and situations that you will encounter.

Even then, an element of luck plays a part, and whatever standard you may be, you need luck, preferably good luck!

To draw the ball stand closed to the target but again aim the clubface where you want the ball to finish.

SHOT-MAKING GUIDE

	Grip	Aim & Alignment	Ball Position	Posture	Weight Distribution	Swing	Ball Flight	Club Choice
Up	normal	right of target	forward	normal	favour right foot	follow contour of slope	goes higher, pull or draw	less lofted
Down	normal	left of target	back	normal	favour left foot	follow contour of slope	lower, push or fade	more lofted
Below	normal	left of target	slightly forward	increase tilt of spine and knee flex	even	steep, out-to-in, little body turn	high, left to right	short to medium iron
Above	normal	right of target	central	decrease tilt of spine	even	flat, good body turn	low, right to left	gentle slope, up to a 5-wood; steeper slope short to medium iron
High	normal	square to open	forward	normal	favour right	upright, increased hand action	high, left to right	as required
Low	normal	square or slightly closed	back of centre	normal	favour left foot	firm wristed, three-quarter punch	low right to left draw	medium to long iron
Rough (low shot)	normal but left hand firmer	square	back	normal	favour left foot	steep arm swing	low with more run	short iron to 5-wood
Rough (high shot)	normal but left hand firmer	open	central	normal	favour left foot	steep arm swing, out-to-in	high, runs on landing	short iron
Divot	normal but firmer	square	back	normal	favour left foot	steep arm swing, three-quarter punch	low	medium to short iron
Slice	weak but firmer left hand	left, clubface at target	forward	normal	even	steeper arm swing, out-to-in	high, left to right	medium to long irons, 3-wood
Draw	stronger, lighter	right, clubface at target	back	normal	even	flatter arm swing, good turn, in-to-out	low, right to left	medium irons

THE SHORT GAME

If you really want to cut your regular score dramatically, improve your short game. There is no reason in the world why women cannot be as good as men in this department since strength has no bearing on the matter. You can also practise in a confined area, such as your garden, or even indoors.

We shall first look at putting, then chipping; both really are the simplest of shots in golf. Each can contribute greatly to your success or downfall since they constitute a fairly high percentage of the shots that are played.

Pitching and bunker shots will follow and if you can learn to get out of a bunker in one shot, then you are on the road to success.

Perhaps one of the hardest aspects of the short game is knowing what shot to play for the occasion, and if you cannot get a clear picture in your mind then you are liable to hit the shot poorly.

Apart from explaining the various departments of the short game, I will endeavour to help you understand how to make the correct choice of shot.

Catrin Nilsmark, the Swedish Solheim Cup player, uses the reverse overlap putting grip to create a firm-wristed action.

PUTTING

The best putters in the world these days use a very passive hand action, where their hands do not work independently of their forearms. In order for this to happen, most of them use a grip called the reverse overlap grip, and I firmly believe that this will enhance most golfers' putting actions.

THE GRIP

The best way to adopt the grip is to place your palms either side of the putter grip square to the target, then close your fingers around the grip, placing both thumbs at the front, not to either side as with the normal golf grip.

Now remove the left forefinger and slide your hands together, allowing the left forefinger to overlap the outside of the right hand fingers.

Clockwise from left: How to take your putting grip. First, place both palms either side of the grip; then close them round the grip but remove the left forefinger. Slide the hands together and overlap the fingers of the right hand with the left forefinger.

The shaft will run more up the centre of the left palm rather than sit under the fleshy pad at the heel of the hand. You will find that this type of grip makes your hands more of a unit, encouraging the back of the left hand to remain firmer throughout the stroke as required.

I personally use a fairly firm grip pressure which I feel helps to keep my hands passive, but many top class players have their hands placed very lightly on the grip. Find out which one works best for you as there is no one right way for all golfers, but do avoid too tight a grip.

THE SET-UP

Whilst it would be true to say that with putting you will see a greater variety of set-ups among good golfers than for other golf shots, certain factors will be common to all, which will encourage the correct action.

Having gripped the club it is important that, as with other shots, you do align the clubface at the target, which of course may not always be the hole, but a spot right or left of it depending on the borrow.

I do the same as on a fairway shot, where I try to aim over something about a foot ahead of the ball on the target line.

On very good blemish free greens this is not always possible, but if direction is your problem, do try to use this method where you can. Align the putter face so that the ball is opposite the sweet spot on the putter, which is usually marked by a line or dot.

With the putter face aimed, take your stance so that you angle forward from the hips. This will allow your arms to hang and swing clear of your body. It is important to keep your shoulders parallel to the target line, but it is more a matter of personal preference whether your feet are square, open or closed.

More good golfers putt with their feet open, but providing the shoulders remain square, the feet are less important. You will encourage a firmer wristed action if you keep the hands high, with the wrists slightly arched.

Ideally, your eyes should be above or just inside the target line. Hang your putter or drop a ball from below your left eye to check this.

Keep your shoulders parallel to the target line, your wrists slightly arched and the putter face aimed at the target.

Keep your hands just ahead of the ball so that the shaft slopes slightly towards the target. The ball is positioned under the left eye.

Ideally your eyes should be over, or just inside the ball, which will give you the best perspective of the putt. Test this either by (a) hanging your putter from under your left eye, or by (b) dropping a ball from beneath the left eye and seeing where it lands. If it hits the ball you are putting or a point just inside, then your head and eye position, and indeed the ball position are fine. If it drops a long way inside, which is fairly common, you may need to angle forward more from the hips, or stand closer to the ball.

Again it is a matter of preference whether your weight is even, or slightly favouring the left foot. Width of stance is also a matter of personal choice, and can vary from very close together to fairly wide. Whichever you choose, try to keep your hands just ahead of the ball so that the shaft slopes a little towards the target, your left eye in line with the ball.

THE STROKE

From this set-up you should swing the putter back so that it stays fairly close to the ground, and makes a very gentle inward arc. On short putts this inward element will not be apparent, and the putter head will go back and through on almost a straight line. But on longer putts the clubhead must start to curve a little inwards on the backswing.

On the throughswing you should endeavour to swing the putter head towards the target, although it will come inside the target line

Right: The putter swings back and through on a very gently curving inward arc, with the putter face square at impact.

slightly, though not as much as on the back-swing. Because of the set-up and consequent stroke, the putter head strikes the ball at the base of the arc or when it is just starting to swing upwards.

Whilst this is how the putter head will travel, in order for this to happen the hands must remain passive, so that the angles at the back of each wrist remain as they were at address. This is especially important to remember at impact and beyond. The body, head and legs should remain very still, so that the whole action looks as though just the arms and shoulders move. I personally feel as though my forearms make the action, my shoulders reacting to this movement. My hands just grip the putter, while the wrists stay firm. If you need more power in the putt, then swing the putter back further and it will accelerate quicker through the ball.

Do not look upon the putting action as a hit, but a stroke. To promote a smooth accelerating action that rolls the ball, try to keep the putter head in contact with the ball as long as you can, and you will take the 'hit' out of the stroke. Always resist the temptation to move your head too early to see where the ball has gone. This is one of the few occasions when I would tell a pupil to keep her head still, and to guess where the ball has finished.

Left: The angles at the back of the wrists remain constant throughout the stroke, producing a smooth action which rolls the ball towards the hole.

FAULTS TO AVOID

Faults in any shot generally originate at address, and this is true for putting. If you stand too upright so that your arms cannot hang free of your body, then the body will be too active and will not allow you to swing the clubhead consistently along the correct path. This is one of the most common faults, so always angle forwards from the hips, then use the test of dropping the ball from beneath the left eye to see how close you are to perfection.

Many golfers aim their body and the clubface right of their target, so that the only way the clubhead can swing towards the target is for them to close the face at impact.

It is quite obvious that this cannot be a very efficient system of putting, and can easily be remedied by practising short putts using two parallel shafts either side of the hole as a guide.

This will make it easy to line up correctly, and then to make the right stroke accordingly. Once this becomes second nature move further away from the hole, and just use one shaft outside the ball as a guide.

On the course try to aim over a target just ahead of the ball wherever possible.

One of the most common faults originates with the hands too far behind the ball at address. From here the arms fail to move an appreciable amount, and a very wristy action is produced, where the back of the left hand bends back on itself at impact and beyond.

There is nothing to commend this, although some golfers, mainly because of the amount of golf they play, may find that they have some reasonable days in spite of it. Please correct this dreadful action now if you recognize it. I can guarantee that you will eventually knock many shots off your score if you jettison this terrible example of a putting stroke.

First check that you use the reverse overlap grip and then keep your hands ahead of the ball at address. The tips on pages 106–107 should help you to attain the correct stroke.

PRACTICE TIPS

Without a club angle forward so that your arms hang relaxed and free of your body, and put your palms together, elbows lightly folded into your sides. Now swing your arms back and through and you will find that your hands and wrists will remain passive, the whole movement coming from your arms and shoulders.

If you can watch yourself in a mirror, you will observe how the triangle of your arms and shoulders stays intact. Whilst you have nothing in your hands, you will not have the tendency to work or move them independently of your arms. Use this exercise whenever you can, even on the golf course during the round.

Take a second club and grip it on the shaft so that it extends under your left arm and up the left side of your body.

As you make the putting action, if your arms stop moving causing your hands to become too active, you will hit yourself in the side with the shaft. You will soon tire of this happening, and it will train you to keep your wrists firm.

I want you to hold the putter with your left hand below the right, all fingers and thumbs on the grip. With the hands in this position, it is much more difficult for the back of the left hand to collapse at impact.

You may have seen players such as Bernhard Langer employing this technique when the more conventional grip has failed them. Practise like this for a short while, then revert to the reverse overlap grip, and you will be able to improve the firmness of your left hand.

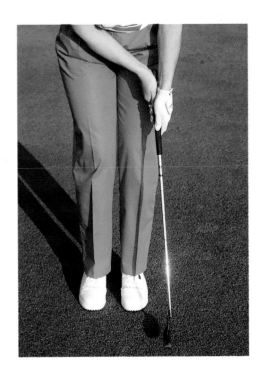

On a gently sloping green, arrange several balls around the hole, starting at about two feet, and try to hole them. This will give a different borrow with each putt. Gradually move outwards about a foot at a time, keeping note how many balls you can hole consecutively.

Start with a few two or three foot putts, then gradually move away from the hole, so that the strike must be pure in order for the ball to drop. To encourage a firm and positive stroke, try to practise slightly uphill putts, perhaps with a little borrow so that you must get the pace and the line correct.

It is vitally important to practise long putts, since not only must you judge the strength of each putt correctly, the actual strike needs to be pure or the ball will finish short of the hole.

Initially, hit several balls to the same target, but then alternate, hitting one ball to each of several targets.

To make the hole seem bigger when you are on the course, practise putting to a much smaller target, like a tee-peg. You'll be surprised at how large the hole will seem after that.

READING THE GREENS

No one can tell you the exact line or how hard to hit a putt; this only comes with experience, allied to a good putting stroke, but there are a few simple guidelines that will improve your ability to read greens correctly. You do not need to be a genius, just observant.

1. On approaching the green observe which way the land around it lies, and it is probable that the green will slope the same way.

2. Try to look at your putt, especially long putts, from sideways on, as this will give you a truer idea of the length than when you stand behind the ball, when distance can be foreshortened.

3. Note whether the grass is a uniform length on each hole, as it does vary, and remember that on faster greens the slope becomes more effective.

4. From behind your ball, look at the hole and decide if the ground about one yard either side slopes, because it is in this area, when the ball is slowing down that it will curve most.

5. Often by walking the length of your putt, your feet will tell you if it is uphill or downhill. As you walk, check the line for stones, sand or pitch marks (which you can mend), so that nothing can deflect the ball.

6. Remember that on downhill putts the ball will take the borrow more than on uphill putts.

7. Watch your partner's ball, and note how it rolls; it may offer some useful information. Also watch your ball if it rolls past the hole as it will tell you the line of the return putt.

I would like to add that any routine you adopt on the green should not become too time consuming. If you are not putting first, most of what I have advised, including mending your own pitch mark, marking and cleaning your ball, and reading the green can be done whilst your partner is preparing to putt.

Look at longer putts from the side to get a better idea of the length.

Watch your putt if it misses the hole as it will give you a good idea of the line of the return putt.

VISUALIZATION

Good putters are those golfers who have the ability to visualize what the ball will do. This is not something that the beginner will instantly accomplish, but it is never too early to develop trying to 'see' the ball rolling across the green.

I can honestly say on many occasions I have had such a clear picture of this happening that the stroke was a mere formality before the ball did, indeed, drop into the hole.

So the better golfers should not just try to get longer putts near the hole, but picture holing them. I firmly believe that for many golfers, it is not precise enough just to lag the ball somewhere close. Focus on the target and you will see your putting improve.

You need to acquire the ability to 'see' the line to the hole.

The beginner may find less pressure by trying to roll the longer putts into an imaginary circle about three feet around the hole. Only by experimenting will you find what makes you achieve your true potential.

FROM OFF THE GREEN

If your ball lies just off the green on the fringe, providing the grass is smooth and even, then it is quite in order to use your putter. Obviously you will have to take into consideration how the longer grass will affect the pace of the putt, but basically you can work on the theory that a bad putt will be safer than a bad chip. Do **not** putt if the ground is very wet or uneven, or the grass is long.

The beauty about putting is that you can practise it indoors, and I know that with even just a little dedication you will find that taking three or four putts is a thing of the past.

Putting from a smooth fringe is the safest shot to play.

CHIPPING

We need, first, to be perfectly clear about the definition of a chip shot. It is a shot played from around the green with an iron, requiring a firm wristed action. It can be played with any iron, depending on the circumstances and to some extent, personal preference. Generally speaking the ball stays fairly low to the ground with chip shots, but this will vary slightly from club to club.

I think it will also help you to improve your chipping if you look upon it as a putt with a lofted club. If you have just read the section on putting, you will be well equipped to learn about chipping, because the actual stroke is the same, although the set-up varies slightly.

THE GRIP

In recent years many professionals have begun using their putting grip (i.e. the reverse overlap) for chipping because, as for putting, it helps to keep the back of the left wrist firm.

You might like to experiment using either this grip or the conventional golf grip. Personally I find the putting grip is superb for very short chip shots, especially to a fast green, since it takes out any hint of extra power that may be produced by the hands. For slightly longer chip shots I would use my normal golf grip. There are no hard and fast rules but it really is worth experimenting.

It is also worth trying different grip pressures; as you do not want the hands to work actively, a slightly firmer grip than usual may prove worthwhile. I am not suggesting a tight grip, but I have found that a firmer grip improves my chipping action and it may do the same for you.

THE SET-UP

With your shoulders parallel to the target line set up with a narrow, open stance, with about 70 per cent of your weight favouring the left foot, positioning your head above your left foot. Play the ball back in the stance well inside the left heel, but keep your hands ahead of the ball so that the shaft slopes towards the target.

It may help you to remember how to set up by thinking of it as two forward and one back,

Set up with more weight on your left side and your hands ahead of the ball, which is played back in the stance.

weight and hands forward, ball back. Grip
down on the club and keep the clubface square
to the target; an interim target about two feet
ahead of the ball may help to this end.

THE SWING

All you have to imagine now is that you are
putting the ball, so that you produce the same
firm-wristed action that I have detailed earlier.
Try to make the backswing and through swing
of similar length, keeping the clubhead fairly
low to the ground and accelerating smoothly
through the ball. There should be little if any
weight transference in the backswing but as you
swing through the right knee will ease towards
the target. Because the set-up is different to
that of a putt, the clubhead will strike the ball
while it is slightly descending, rather than at
the base of the arc or just on the upswing.

As with putting, avoid looking up too quickly
as this will cause poor contact. Look at the ball,
then at the piece of grass on which it sat, and
guess how close you have hit it.

If you have a very bad lie where the ball sits
in a depression or on bare ground, I suggest that
you play the ball back in the stance opposite
the inside of your right foot. This will enable
you to make a more descending strike on the
ball, which is needed in this instance. This
set-up reduces the loft on the club, so you may
need to use a more lofted club to compensate,
or simply allow for this in the shot.

If the lie is very good, and you are a fairly
competent golfer, you may get a better rolling
action if you play the ball forward in the stance
opposite the left heel. This set-up adds loft to
the club, so you may need to play a straighter
faced club, or simply allow for this in the shot.

The chipping stroke is very similar to that used for putting.
Let the clubface get the ball airborne.

Faults to Avoid

FAULT

With regard to the actual stroke, the most common fault is the same as in putting, when the whole action becomes too wristy, so that the hands are too active instead of passive.

Usually this is caused by a bad set up where the ball is too far forward, the weight is too even, and the hands are too far back. The arms fail to move enough, and the action hinges from the wrists, so that at impact the left wrist collapses back on itself. You are liable either to thin the shot so that the ball charges across the green and probably off the other side, or you may hit it fat so that it goes nowhere.

CURE

To cure this, first check the set up using a mirror to help, then use the same three practice putting tips that are detailed on pages 106 and 107.

CHOICE OF CLUB

The main idea with chipping is to select a club that will land the ball about a yard or two on the green, from where it will run up to, or hopefully into the hole. I suggested that for long putts a sideways look would be a good idea to help judge distance, and the same is true for chipping, where you must first visualize how the ball should travel; does it need to be in the air more than on the ground, or vice versa? Based on what you see, you should select the correct club to help you play the shot.

If you are perhaps fifteen yards from the green with the hole cut just five yards on, this type of shot would be best played with a lofted club, so that the ball will spend most of its journey in the air.

Alternatively, if you are just a few yards from the edge of the green with the hole about twenty yards away, then a straighter-faced club, possibly a 6- or 7-iron would be preferable.

I know many professionals tend to favour one club for chipping, and this is often a wedge or sand iron. They vary the ball position according to the situation to produce different shots. This is not how the beginner should approach chipping; she would be best to use probably just two clubs, a wedge and a 7-iron. The 7-iron can be used in most instances, even, providing the ground is not very soft and wet, to land the ball well short of the green for a long chip and run shot. Use the wedge when the pin is close to your side of the green to produce a more lofted shot. If you are a newcomer to the game, you are aiming to strike the ball correctly in the right direction, even if the distance is somewhat erratic.

The more advanced golfer will have become familiar with how the ball reacts with different clubs in different situations, perhaps using any

From well off the green use a fairly lofted club as the ball must carry to the green.

club from a 5-iron to a sand wedge. If you have never chipped with the sand wedge, try it sometime when you are on the fringe with little green to work with.

If you are only just off the green a straighter faced club will get the ball over the fringe and running well towards the hole.

CHIPPING FROM ROUGH

If the ball sits down a little in greenside rough, you will need to change the chipping action so that the clubhead does not get caught up in the grass and clean contact is made with the ball.

The clubhead must approach from a steeper attack, so play the ball further back in the stance than usual, the exact position depending on the lie. Keep the weight on the left side, your hands well ahead of the clubhead, but with the clubface square to the target. Lift the clubhead up steeply in the backswing by cocking the wrists almost immediately, then hit down and through.

It is more difficult to be accurate from poor lies, but the ball should come out low and run. It requires almost a stabbing action, but do not quit at the ball, but hit through it, keeping the back of the left wrist firm.

Because this set-up naturally reduces the effective loft of the club, a sand iron or wedge are usually the best clubs to use.

Dottie Mochrie has no fear of chipping over a bunker because to her the bunker does not exist.

OVER A BUNKER

When chipping from the rough you will need an early wrist break on the take-away.

For many golfers hitting a short shot over a bunker is a nightmare. Because so many players lack confidence with the shot, they play it too quickly, lift their heads too soon, and have the wrong picture of how the stroke should be played. Although the better golfer or professional may use a more wristy type of pitch shot in this situation, providing I had a reasonable lie, if my life depended on it, I would probably play the shot using a firm wristed action.

With a sand iron, set up in the same way as for a normal chip shot but with the stance just a little wider. Simply swing back and through watching the turf a little longer than usual. Allow your weight to transfer to the right on a descending strike. The ball may not fly as high as it would with a more wristy shot, but it is a more reliable method for most golfers.

Practise this shot as it will improve your skill and aid your confidence.

the backswing and to the left on the through swing, so that your knees move in harmony with your arms and body. There is nothing too difficult about it other than judging how hard to hit it. It is usually preferable to hit too hard rather than too soft and risk going in the bunker.

You **must** practise this, ideally over a bunker, but if not try hitting over your golf bag. Visualize the clubhead swinging down slightly on the ball, **never** think of hitting the ball **up** into the air, because this usually causes the clubhead to be swinging upwards at impact rather than downwards. If you have no success at first, give yourself good lies, and play the ball a little further back in your stance to encourage

THE LONG CHIP AND RUN

By lengthening the swing, but still using what feels like the chipping action you will be able to play a long chip and run shot, especially useful on links courses and in windy conditions. In the backswing you may find the wrists break a little, and the right elbow starts to fold, which is natural. There will also be more body and leg action as the weight transfers back and through. Be certain, though, that your wrists stay firm through impact and keep the left arm moving throughout.

For a long chip and run shot lengthen your swing but keep the wrists firm through impact.

You should look upon the chip shot as an extension of putting, allowing the loft on the club to send the ball into the air and over the fringe. Practise as often as you can, and if your course does not have a practice chipping green, chipping from a coconut mat in your garden is better than nothing. You might also ask your club why they do not have a chipping green!

PRACTICE TIPS

To enable you to learn how the ball reacts with different clubs, using the same strength of swing, hit about ten shots with each of the even numbered clubs including the wedge, and you will find that the ball spends less time in the air and rolls further with the lower numbered clubs than it does with the higher numbered ones.

Consequently, even though you use the same strength swing, a 4-iron will hit the ball further than an 8-iron. This drill only informs you how the ball reacts with these clubs, which is vital knowledge though it does not assist you with how hard to hit the ball.

The following brief summary of the air time/roll time ratio, may be useful.

7-iron: one-third air, two-thirds roll.
9-iron: one half air, one half roll.
wedge: two-thirds air, one-third roll.

These are only approximate ratios, since ground conditions vary enormously and will affect how the ball reacts on landing.

Take one club and chip to different holes to improve your judgment of distance. Hit only one ball to each hole, as it is too easy to get it right second time; on the course you do not have a second chance.

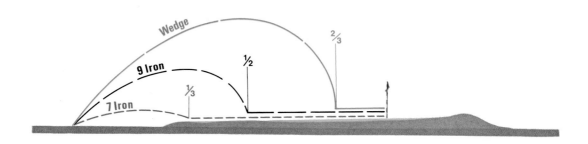

To help you judge how far back to swing your arms, use the clockface again, but this time imagine that it is upright, with your feet at 6 o'clock, and your head at 12 o'clock. Practise swinging your arms back to perhaps 8 o'clock using a 7-iron, noting how far the ball rolls.

Then swing back to 7 o'clock and see how the distance has been affected. Although this will not instantly make you able to hit the ball the correct distance, it will help you estimate more precisely the length of swing required.

For the more advanced player, when you practise remember that you are not trying to get the ball near the hole, you are trying to get it **in** the hole. This holds true on the course too; raise your expectations and you may raise your standard of play. If you are going to hole a chip, the ball must have enough power to at least reach the hole, so this will make you more positive in your approach.

PITCHING

The pitch shot is played to get maximum height and stop on the ball, therefore the main clubs to use are the wedge and sand wedge. The shot differs from a chip in that a steep angle of attack is created using more wrist and hand action, which means the shot needs slightly better coordination. It is generally used to play over bunkers or trees, or from further away to put additional backspin on the ball for control.

The stance for this shot is narrow and open, but the shoulders remain parallel to the target, with the hands just ahead of the ball.

THE SHORT PITCH

This is the shot usually played over a bunker around the green, and is perhaps one of the most disliked shots in golf for the beginner. It is jokingly called a NITBY – meaning Not In The Bunker Yet! But please don't let that thought ever enter your head, because I can assure you that negative thoughts lead to negative actions, so think positive.

Florence Descampe plays the short pitch to perfection in the BMW European Masters.

A little earlier I showed you how to play a chip and run shot using a sand wedge or a wedge, which are quite suitable for this type of situation, especially for the beginner or for someone whose short game is not very good. The action that I am now going to describe requires a more upward arm swing than for the chip and run shot, and as a result a steeper attack on the ball, which generally gives more height and consequently less run to the shot. Therefore, depending on the situation, and your ability, you could choose either method.

Whilst the shoulders remain parallel to the target the stance is open and narrow, with the ball being played just inside the left foot, just a little further forward than for a chip and run shot.

As for all short shots the weight favours the left foot, and you must ensure that your head is more above this foot than the right. The hands should be just ahead of the ball so that the shaft slopes slightly towards the target.

If the lie is poor, with the ball sitting down, it would be advisable to play it further back in the stance.

Although this will reduce the effective loft of the club, it will help to guarantee a better downward contact. Grip down on the club, making sure that you do so by about the same amount each time. If you vary this you are in effect using a different club every time and this does not make the judgment of distance any easier.

Concentrate on swinging your forearms **up** away from the ball, so that the clubhead swings steeply. Although I have said that pitching has more hand action than chipping, you should not consciously pick the clubhead up with your hands. Make your forearms the main motors and you will find that as the right elbow folds, so the wrists will naturally hinge. There will be a little weight transference onto the right foot and some shoulder turn.

the impact zone, the back of the left hand remains firm, almost facing the sky as the right hands works underneath it rather than rotating over it as in the normal golf swing.

Because of this, as the left elbow folds it moves backwards rather than downwards as in the full swing.

At impact keep the back of the left wrist moving towards the target, holding the blade open.

As the forearms swing up, fold the right elbow and the wrists will cock naturally.

The left elbow moves backwards, keeping the blade facing the sky.

Having swung your forearms up, all you need to do now is swing them **down**, feeling that you **pull** the clubhead back to the ball. As this happens your weight must smoothly move back onto the left foot. You should have the feeling of keeping your hands **ahead** of the clubhead at impact. To keep the clubface square through

The legs must work towards the target to permit this type of action. Be sure to watch the ball, then the turf long enough, so that you do not raise your head and your body too early and encourage poor shots. Because the shoulders are square at address the swing path is from in-to-in. Try to make the backswing and through swing about the same length, so that good rhythm is also created.

You must **never** think of hitting the ball up into the air, but picture the clubhead descending onto the ball, or into the turf, and the ball will be lofted quite easily.

The more advanced and better golfer could use a swing where the wrists cock quite early in the backswing, producing a shot where the ball flies a little higher. But be certain that (a) this action is supported by the forearms swinging and, (b) the left wrist is firm at impact.

Try to make the backswing and throughswing the same length, finishing balanced on the left side.

VARYING LENGTH AND HEIGHT

I believe that it is best to vary the length of the shot by varying the length of the swing, keeping the pace and rhythm the same. By this I mean that the further you wish to hit the ball, the longer the backswing should become, thus creating more natural momentum through impact.

To give you a better idea of how to regulate this, use the clock face as we did for chipping, i.e. imagine it is vertical with your feet at 6 o'clock, and your head at 12 o'clock. By swinging your arms back say to 8, 9, or 10 o'clock, and through the corresponding amount, the distance of the shot will increase with each hour. You will need to practise this with your wedge and sand wedge until you become familiar with how far each 'hour' hits the ball, but by having a more precise length of swing in mind you will hit many more positive pitches.

Use the clock face to help you with the length of your shots.

Playing the ball forward will help you increase the loft on the shot.

With a very short pitch, you will find it helps to go further down the grip than usual, thus instantly diminishing the power of the club. By the same token, for longer shots you may need to grip the club almost at full length. However, I would reiterate that for most shots you should try to go down the grip about the same amount, so that you are using a club with an equal amount of built-in power each time.

There are two main methods of varying the height on the shot; you can either play the ball further forward in your stance, or open the clubface a little more than normal.

You can really only play the ball forward, perhaps two inches nearer the left foot, if the lie is good with a decent cushion of grass beneath the ball so that the clubhead can slide under it. If you choose this method, keep your hands a little behind the ball so that the clubface has maximum loft. Keep the weight even and try to slide the clubhead under the ball, keeping the clubface square as before. This is not the shot for the high handicapper, nor the shot for the better golfer to play too often. If it goes wrong, you could thin the ball with disastrous results.

If you open your shoulders and the clubface you will gain extra height on the shot, but you will have to hit the ball harder than usual to get the required length. This, of course, needs some

practice, and whilst the shot itself is not too difficult, played the same as for other pitch shots, problems can arise with knowing exactly how much to open the shoulders and clubface, and determining the power required. There is also the danger of hitting a shank shot, as this part of the clubhead is leading into the ball first.

I would suggest that by using a square set-up with a sand iron you should normally be able to get sufficient height on the majority of your shots, only using an open position when the pin is very close to your side of the green, and you must get down in two shots.

One word of warning about the sand iron; if the ground is very firm avoid using it as the flange will tend to bounce off the turf causing you to thin the ball. Instead settle for using a wedge which has a sharper leading edge and narrower sole which will cope better with this particular situation.

Professionals practise these shots for hours, whilst the club golfer would rarely think of doing so. You must be certain that you are capable of a shot before attempting it on the course, so a little practice goes a long way.

For extra height, open your shoulders and the clubface.

THE LONG PITCH

For the more advanced golfer the long pitch shot, perhaps in excess of sixty yards or so, offers the opportunity to strike the ball with a more punchy action and so impart increased backspin.

When performed by the best players in the world, this is the shot that spins backwards on the green. However, certain circumstances must prevail in order for this to happen.

Firstly the lie must be good with little or no grass between the clubface and ball at impact, and secondly a Balata ball must be used as this has a soft cover and spins quicker than a Surlyn covered ball. The problem is that the Balata cover also cuts more easily, and exaggerates any unwanted slice or hook, so is not ideal for the club golfer.

Finally the green needs to be receptive, not very firm as many courses are in summer.

You could use a sand.iron, wedge or even a 9-iron, depending on the length, but please remember that the short irons are for accuracy, and trying to hit them too hard will not enhance this aspect.

The right hand strikes against a firm left wrist to promote backspin.

SET-UP AND SWING

Your shoulders should be parallel to the target line with the feet and hips a little open, stance wider than for the short pitch, but not too wide, weight favouring the left foot. The ball is played inside the left heel, hands ahead of the ball, and shaft just sloping towards the target.

Although there is some body turn, it is predominantly the arms that make the backswing by swinging upwards away from the ball, while the weight transfers a little. From the top of the backswing the arms, especially the left, must have the feeling of pulling the clubhead back to the ball, but just at impact the right hand provides a definite punch, while the back of the left hand and wrist remain firm, and facing the target. The follow through is somewhat curtailed, the weight having transferred back onto the left side through impact.

The beginner who may find this action quite difficult should simply play a normal short iron shot with the appropriate club, concentrating on swinging the clubhead down into the ball.

Be realistic, play the shot that guarantees hitting the ball onto the green, and not one that you have little chance of executing well.

The long pitch requires a fuller backswing and wider stance.

CHOOSING THE RIGHT SHOT

One of the most important points about choosing which shot to play around the greens is to play one which you are most confident of executing correctly. Naturally this confidence can usually only develop through practice and experience, so be patient and realistic.

One of the easy guides to remember is not to play a chip shot if you can putt, and not pitch the ball if you can chip it. It is always easier to putt than chip, and easier to chip than pitch.

Always try to visualize what route ideally the ball has to take to finish near (or in) the hole, then select the club that will make the shot possible. For instance, you would not use a 7-iron to hit the ball over a bunker, nor should you try to play a long low chip and run shot with a sand iron.

Certainly as you progress you will become more proficient at some shots than others, but until such time as practice has enlarged your repertoire, then you should play the shot you know. Most ladies tend to play a long chip and run shot with a club like a 7-iron from much further off the green than I would. They run the risk of the ball being thrown off line by some slope or mound on the fairway, but this, for them, is a risk worth taking, as they will almost certainly get the ball somewhere on the green.

The more advanced golfer would be far better playing a more lofted club so that the ball almost always lands on the green, thus ensuring a more predictable bounce.

This is a slightly more difficult shot but, if correctly executed, will give them a better chance of getting the ball close to the hole and not just on the green. Try to watch good golfers, or even caddy for a good player in your club matches if possible because you will learn a lot from their choice of shot, and how they play it.

This illustration gives you a good idea of the amount of air-time different clubs have, and where they may best be used. By choosing the right club for different shots around the green you will make it easier to get the ball close to, or even in the hole.

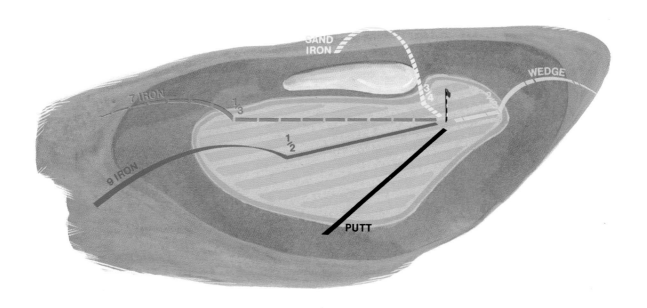

FAULTS TO AVOID

The main fault that the beginner has is falling back onto the right side at impact in an effort to scoop the ball into the air. This in fact has precisely the opposite result, as the ball is invariably topped. That merely encourages the player to try even harder to scoop the ball up.

One of the easiest ways to cure this is to practise with only the tips of the toes of the right foot on the ground and the weight mainly on the left foot. This set-up will encourage the clubhead to swing **downwards** onto the ball, and it is impossible to fall back onto the right side. Have a definite picture of the clubhead descending, making several practice swings, taking a divot of grass from virtually opposite the left foot.

For the short pitch, the swing can become too hand orientated, so that excessive power is built into the shot. The hands contain the fast moving muscles of the body, and therefore when you are trying to produce a shot with little power or speed, it makes sense to keep them quiet. The golfer who pitches in this way also lacks consistency of strike and length of shot.

If this is your problem, I would suggest that you make the swing much more forearm orientated, letting the hands remain passive. Reread the end of the chipping section, regarding playing over a bunker (page 116). In this shot I used and advised an extended chipping action, where the wrists only slightly start to cock, and this type of swing would make you much more consistent at playing the short pitch shots around the green.

Judgment of distance is the key to good pitching, and more often than not shots are left very short of the hole. Providing there is no great trouble over the back of the green, or by going past the pin you would not leave yourself a very awkward downhill putt, be determined to hit the ball at least pin high, if not past the hole. Earlier I suggested that using the clockface as a guide to backswing length would help to judge distance, so do spend some time practising this method, because I **know** it will help.

Bunkers

In my experience of teaching and playing in many pro-ams, it is lack of ability in playing bunker shots that is the Achilles heel of most club golfers. The reason basically stems from poor technique, often brought about by having the wrong picture in mind of how the shot should be played.

Bad technique leads to lack of confidence, and so the shot is usually rushed, the player trusting to luck as to whether the ball comes out or not. Few clubs have a good practice bunker, so even for those who wish to work on this aspect of their game, conditions do not always make it easy.

To play bunker shots well you must have the correct picture in mind of what you are trying to do, you must practise as much as possible, then apply your new technique on the course.

Please bear this in mind; to play bunker shots consistently well, you must remove a shallow divot of sand about six to eight inches long from around the ball, and the ball will fly out of the bunker on this divot. The clubhead must enter the sand about two inches behind the ball. It is the downward action of the clubhead that will send the ball into the air.

Alison Nicholas shows the full follow through necessary to splash the ball out of a bunker first time.

THE SET-UP

The club to use for most bunker shots is a sand iron, which is specially designed with an extra piece of metal on the sole called the flange, which prevents the clubhead digging too deeply into the sand. For the flange to be most effective the clubface must be turned **open first**, then gripped. If you grip it first, with the clubface square, and then open it, at impact your hands will return to a neutral position and the face will thus be square. So remember, open the clubface first, then grip it. It will also help you to grip down a little for extra control.

The beginner may find it helpful to take her grip outside the bunker, since the clubhead may not touch the sand at all before impact.

Turn the clubface open, then grip the club, going down the grip a little for extra control.

You must set up with your shoulders, hips, knees and feet open to the line of the target, the feet slightly more open than the shoulders. The clubface should aim a little to the right of the target. This address position will create the steep out-to-in swing which, together with the open clubface, will cause the ball to fly high, with very little power. The ball should be positioned forward in a fairly narrow stance, approximately opposite the left instep, with the weight about 60 per cent on the left foot.

Wriggle your feet securely into the sand, taking notice of the depth and texture. The hands should still be just ahead of the ball with the shaft sloping slightly towards the target. Better players and professionals may play some shots from good lies with their hands level with, or even just behind the ball, but if you are a beginner, or unsuccessful at bunker shots, keep your hands just ahead. You **must not** let the club touch the sand prior to impac, so let it hover **above** the entry point in the sand, which should be about two inches behind the ball. Focus on this spot, and **not** the ball.

THE SWING

The swing is made predominantly by the arms swinging up and down, with less emphasis on a shoulder turn. Some weight transference occurs, especially on longer shots, but the swing should feel arm orientated, with the wrists cocking. At the top of the backswing the club shaft will point left of the target.

From the top of the backswing the arms must pull the clubhead back to the ball, retaining the wrist cock as the weight transfers back onto the left side. The left arm must play a major role, pulling the clubhead through the sand so that

Set up open to the target.

The weight favours the left side, hands just ahead of the ball, the club held above the entry point in the sand.

the clubface does not close. The right hand must **not** rotate over the left at impact, so that as you swing through it works under the right, the clubface pointing almost skywards.

It is very important that you swing **through** to a balanced finish or else there is a danger that you will allow the resistance of the sand to slow the clubhead down so much that you leave the ball in the bunker. Finish with the weight on the left foot, and your body facing the target much as it would be for a full iron shot from the fairway.

Providing you swing along the line of your shoulders, this set-up automatically dictates that the club swings across the target line. In clock face terms, imagining that the target is still at 9 o'clock, the club swings from about 2.30 to 8.30. This will naturally send the ball high, usually with quite a lot of backspin so that it will stop fairly quickly.

Always keep the swing smooth, and remember to swing **through** the sand, not **at** the ball. The shot is called a splash shot, not a blast, so think of splashing the ball out rhythmically. It really is a pitch from sand, where the clubhead hits the sand first instead of the ball.

VARYING THE LENGTH

To vary the length of shot the best bunker players in the world tend to use a combination of factors, as follows:

(a) keeping the set-up consistent, they alter the length and therefore the power of the swing;

(b) they vary the amount they open the club-face and stance;

Above, left to right: The bunker swing in sequence. Take the club away fairly steeply, with little shoulder turn. At the top of the backswing the club is pointing well left of the target. The left arm pulls the club down towards impact.

Below: At impact the weight is transferring to the left, the right hand staying under the left, not releasing as for a normal shot. Finish facing the target, the weight on the left side.

(c) they vary the amount of sand taken before the ball.

Depending on the lie and circumstances, they make these adjustments almost automatically, but they have, I can assure you, spent many many hours practising, so that these adjustments are second nature to them. However, my recommendation for the club golfer is mainly to use method (a) so that you make adjustments to the length of swing, much as you would for a pitch shot. This way the set-up stays constant and becomes more familiar to you. Once you reach the limits using this method, then you will have to use methods (b) and (c) according to the situation.

A word of advice for the beginner, and for those who hate bunker shots. First, learn one basic shot where you swing your hands back to at least shoulder height in the backswing, then accelerate smoothly through the sand. This should send the ball about ten to fifteen yards, which ought to be satisfactory for most situations. Only when you become proficient at this should you start to vary the length of the swing, because the main danger, especially with very short shots, is that you do not hit through the sand due to the resistance it offers.

American Beth Daniel stands very open to play a short bunker shot.

When the ball is plugged, play it back in your stance, the clubface and stance square.

PLUGGED LIES

If the ball is plugged in the sand, square the stance and the clubface and position the ball centrally in your stance, or even slightly back of centre for a very bad lie. Keep the weight on the left side and hands well ahead of the ball.

This set-up reduces the effective loft of the club so the ball will not come out as high as with a splash shot. Swing your arms up steeply, cocking the wrists, then hit down into the sand about one inch behind the ball. You will not be able to follow through very much and the ball will come out low and run, so be careful with your aim, as you do not want to run across the green into another bunker.

With the spine at right angles to the slope, keep the weight on the right foot.

With a poor lie always be grateful to get out in one shot, even backwards or sideways if going straight at the pin looks too daunting.

If the ball is plugged in the bunker face, there are two escape methods.

First, try to stand with the spine at right angles to the slope, weight on the right foot, ball forward in your stance. Keep the set-up and clubface fairly square to the target; you will

naturally have maximum loft on the clubface from this type of set-up, which is the same as for an uphill lie from the fairway. Hit firmly into the sand about an inch behind the ball and it will come out high with little forward roll.

Secondly, when the slope is so severe that the above set-up is impossible, lean into the slope with the weight on the left foot, ball inside the left heel, clubface open, then hit into the sand

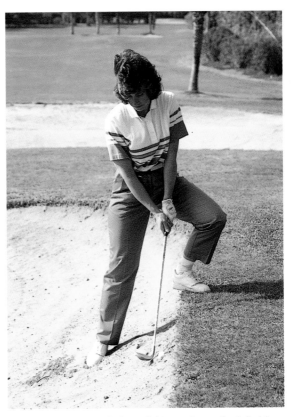

With the spine vertical, the weight remains on the left side, the clubface open.

about one inch behind the ball. You will not be able to follow through as the club will bury itself in the bunker face, but the ball should come out fairly easily.

With each of these methods take a wider stance than usual to help keep your balance, and have a practice swing without touching the sand so that you are familiar with how the shot will feel.

WET OR FIRMLY PACKED SAND

When the sand is in this condition, it becomes far more difficult for the clubhead to penetrate it, and the wide sole can often bounce off the sand sending the leading edge of the club into the back of the ball, thinning it out quite violently.

To counteract this do not open the clubface but keep it, and the set-up square to the target. With the ball more central in your stance, your weight on the left side, aim to contact the sand nearer the ball, about one inch behind it.

Think only of hitting **down** firmly through the sand, and the ball should come out. You may get improved results with a pitching wedge, as its sharper leading edge is better able to cut through the sand.

SLOPING LIES IN SAND

Sadly, by the very nature of their design, you will not always find the ball resting on a flat lie in a bunker, and certain adjustments, much the same as those for shots from sloping fairways, must be made. In these instances, you must always try to swing in a balanced fashion, never looking up too early to see the results of your efforts.

UPHILL LIES

Stand with the spine at right angles to the slope, your weight on the right foot, the ball forward. Keep the set up and clubface fairly square to the target; you will naturally have maximum loft on the clubface from this type of set-up. Hit firmly into the sand about one inch behind the ball, and it will come out high with little forward roll. Try to swing the clubhead along the contours of the sand.

The ball here is more forward, the spine at right angles to the slope.

DOWNHILL LIES

These are among the most difficult shots in golf, where the ball often lies near the back of the bunker, and you have a steep face in front of you. Unfortunately the correct set-up reduces the effective loft of the clubface, and so the task is not made easier.

Until you have practised these shots it may be better to play out sideways or backwards, but let me tell you how to play the shot correctly, so that you know what to practise.

Use an early wrist-cock in the backswing to avoid hitting the sand, then swing your arms up steeply with little shoulder turn.

The spine is at right angles to the slope, the weight on the left side and the ball back in the stance.

The set-up is virtually the same as for a downhill shot from the fairway. The spine should be set at right angles to the slope by placing the weight on the left foot, making sure that your head feels above this foot as well.

Your left shoulder will feel much lower than usual, the shoulders being almost horizontal. The ball is played back in the stance and the clubface should be only slightly open. If you open it too much, there is the danger that the clubhead will not penetrate the sand, just bounce off the surface ineffectively

As you swing your arms up, you must cock your wrists almost immediately so that the clubhead does not hit the sand. The most important picture to keep in mind is to swing the club head down the slope, entering the sand about two inches behind the ball. Your right knee must work through the shot to allow this to happen.

Continue looking down at the sand an extra second or two. The ball will come out low and run, so do not attempt this shot from a severe downhill lie with a six feet bank ahead.

Be certain to swing the clubhead down the contour of the sand.

Do **not** be tempted to fall back onto the right foot in an effort to hit the ball into the air, just let the clubhead do the work. By trial and error you will know when to play this shot, and when to play out sideways. I have seen the best in the world do just that when they know that to aim at the green is attempting the impossible.

SIDEHILL LIES

You make basically the same adjustments for these as for shots from the fairway, which means it is the posture and swing plane that alter. Whilst, when the ball is above the feet, the shot is not too difficult (except in extreme circumstances), when the ball is below the feet, you are facing one of the most difficult shots in golf. Sometimes you may find that the ball is in the bunker, but you have to stand outside, which means that you must take enough time to decide how best to stand and to play it.

BALL ABOVE FEET

When the ball is above your feet, grip down the club, stand a little more upright and play the ball slightly more centrally. The swing will be flatter than for normal bunker shots and you should aim a little right of the target as the ball is likely to be pulled left. In extreme circumstances, when the ball might be almost shoulder height, you may need to grip almost down to the metal shaft to help you play the shot.

With the ball above your feet grip down the club more and remember to aim slightly right of your target.

It would be helpful to make a few practice swings without touching the sand so that you become familiar with the feel of the shot.

This and the downhill shot certainly rank among the hardest in golf, so once again it's practice that is required.

With the ball below your feet wriggle your feet down more to get a good balance.

BALL BELOW FEET

When the ball is below the feet, grip nearer the end of the club, angle forward more from the hips and increase the knee flex. It will also help if you wriggle your feet deeper into the sand, taking a wider stance than normal.

Do not aim as far left as usual, because this set-up will naturally make you swing across the ball from out-to-in. The swing is made mainly by the arms swinging up and down.

You must retain the original spinal angle and your balance, or you will top, thin or shank the shot, so do not swing too hard, and watch the sand a little longer than usual.

LONG BUNKER SHOTS

Whatever length of bunker shot you are faced with, getting out at the first attempt is the major priority. According to your ability this will mean that more than one option may present itself, and only through playing experience, and practice can you become certain that you are attempting a shot within your capabilities.

Long bunker shots are among the most difficult to play, and the golfer must always determine whether it is safe to risk getting the distance instead of the height. The beginner is always better off making certain that she gets enough height on the shot to get out first time, whilst for the more advanced player the gamble is less of a risk. You can use a sand iron, wedge or 9-iron depending on the situation and your strength.

Set up only slightly open, keeping the clubface aimed square to or just right of the target. Wriggle your feet into the sand just enough to get a firm foothold, and grip down the club a corresponding amount.

Providing the ball is sitting up on the sand, you want to hit it first, so play it more centrally than for the splash bunker shot, virtually as you would a pitch shot. From then on focus on the back of the ball and play the shot using mainly the arms and shoulders, keeping the swing, particularly the change of direction, very smooth.

Keep the foot and leg action quiet as even the slightest loss of footing can result in poor contact being made on the ball.

If the ball is lying down in the sand, you will have to hit the sand first, thus losing some power and distance. In this instance you may have to settle for a less than perfect shot, being content to get the ball out at the first attempt.

By using a wedge or 9-iron you will gain more distance, but be sure that the bunker face is not too high.

Practise using different clubs in different situations until you learn your limits. Always bear in mind that to increase the distance you can either set the stance and clubface squarer to the target, hit nearer the ball, or hit the ball itself. You could also either swing longer or use a more powerful club.

For long bunker shots set up squarer to the target and play the ball more towards the centre of your stance. Your aim is to take the ball off the sand cleanly.

FAIRWAY BUNKERS

Although you want distance from these shots, getting out in one must be the major aim, so you must select a club that will safely hit the ball high enough to miss the face of the bunker.

Look at the shot from the side to get a better perspective, then take one club less than you think is playable, e.g. a 6-iron instead of a 5, so that you have room for error. Wriggle your feet slightly into the sand, and grip down the club a corresponding amount.

Play the ball slightly more central in a square stance, and use a smooth, firm wristed swing, perhaps three-quarters length and power at most. Ideally you will hit the ball first, then the sand, so look more towards the top of the ball rather than the back of it.

Even a few grains of sand taken before contacting the ball will dampen the effect of the swing, so do not be too ambitious with the escape route you choose. If the ball is lying very well, a fairway wood will often get a good result.

Grip down the club for extra control, play the ball just inside the left heel and sweep it off the top of the sand. You must only attempt this shot when there is little or no lip on the bunker, and the ball lies central or back in the bunker. Keep your balance and swing smoothly, keeping the transition from the backswing to the downswing unhurried.

BAD LIES

If the ball sits down in a fairway bunker and the face is not high, you can attempt one of two shots, either (a) play a normal splash shot using any club between a sand iron and a 7-iron, contacting the sand about one inch behind the ball, or (b) play the ball back of centre in the stance, hands ahead of the ball, with the set-up and clubface square, weight favouring the left side. This set-up encourages the necessary steep attack. Use a predominantly arm and shoulder swing, with little weight transference. Aim to contact the sand about one inch behind the ball and swing through as much as possible.

I would suggest that you use method (a) when the ball is not lying too badly, and method (b) when it is lying deeper in the sand.

Hitting from a fairway bunker you need to take the ball off cleanly, with no sand. A fairway wood is ideal for this as it will not dig into the sand.

With a bad lie, play the ball back of centre of your stance with the weight on the left side.

PRACTICE TIPS

Check your set-up, because this can be the root cause of your problems. In a practice bunker, draw a line from the ball towards the target, then draw a line that aims to the left of it, in clock face terms at about 8.30, and a line at a right angle from the ball. Then use these lines to practise addressing the ball correctly, setting your shoulders parallel to the 8.30 line and your feet a little open to it, making sure that the line at right angles to the target is opposite the left instep or heel. The clubface should aim just right of target.

Because greenside bunker shots are usually not very long, the temptation is to make a short backswing, which means that you will not have enough momentum to swing through the sand, which offers great resistance to the clubhead's progression. I know that a short swing often develops because on occasions, when the ball has been contacted first rather than the sand, the ball has flown too far, often into trouble.

So you must improve your clubhead control. A very good exercise for this is to draw two parallel lines in the sand about six to eight inches apart, at right angles to the target line.

Stand with the right hand line about two inches inside the left heel, then try to remove a divot of sand from between the lines.

This exercise will not only inform you of your accuracy of strike, but will help make you concentrate on the sand and not the ball.

Having the wrong picture in mind, many golfers try to hit the ball up into the air, and fall back onto their right foot in an effort to do so.

This only has the effect of either contacting the sand too far behind the ball, thus diminishing the power of the strike, or hitting the ball cleanly, which means it will go too far. Neither is acceptable, so the picture of what you are trying to do must be changed so that you imagine the clubhead going **down** into the sand.

The previous exercise would be helpful, together with the following. Set up with the weight on the left foot, then place just the toe of your right shoe in the sand. From this set-up it is difficult to fall back onto the right foot.

When you swing from a normal set-up, be sure that you start with your weight on your left side, keeping it there through impact, and finish balanced facing the target.

ON THE COURSE

Before I explain anything about golf course strategy, I would like to highlight the need for you to observe golfing etiquette.

Thankfully, golf remains one of the few sports where courtesy and consideration for others is still paramount.

For those who have played the game for many years, etiquette becomes second nature, but for the beginner it is important to adhere to certain rules right from the start. Do not be offended by anyone telling you that you have forgotten certain courtesies as we all have to learn, and it is the responsibility of those familiar with these traditions to ensure they are perpetuated.

Observe the following and you will readily be accepted on a golf course.

1. Remain still and silent when others are playing.
2. Stand so that you and your equipment are out of vision of the person playing her shot.
3. Be ready to play when it is your turn.
4. Keep up with the pace of play, and call faster players through if necessary, particularly if you lose a ball or lag behind the group in front.
5. Repair pitch marks on the green, (even if they are not yours); replace divots, and rake bunkers.

6. Do not tread on your partners' line on the green.
7. Attend the pin if asked, but do not stand too close to the hole.
8. Do not play until those in front are out of range.
9. Shout 'fore' when the ball is in the air if you have hit it towards others.
10. When you are on the green, leave your clubs en route to the next tee.
11. Do not place your golf bag or trolley on the green or tee.
12. Do not walk close to players who are swinging, or swing towards other players.
13. Do not throw clubs; it is rude and you look ridiculous.

These rules are more important than your standard of golf, and ensure that everyone has a fair chance to play the course in comfort.

PREPARING TO PLAY

Go to any professional tournament and you will see the players warming up by hitting shots before they play.

Wisely, they are gradually easing their muscles into action, and getting the feel of the swing for that day. In contrast, most amateurs arrive with barely enough time to tie their shoelaces, rush onto the tee and proceed to duff shots until they, too, have warmed up their muscles after several holes.

Whilst I would readily accept that it is not

realistic for most players to hit shots before they play, do try to allow yourself at least ten to fifteen minutes just to gently swing a club, and hopefully have a few putts.

Check you have enough tees and golf balls, and that you do not have more than fourteen clubs in your bag. If you are playing in an important competition, do try to hit some shots before you play, even if it is just a few short iron shots. Do not rush, but arrive on the first tee with enough time to compose yourself. A few deep breaths will help you to relax.

All professionals spend some time warming up before a round of golf. If you can make time to hit a few dozen balls on the practice range first, your game will benefit.

PLANNING YOUR ROUND

Golf is a strategic game, where you must try to plan your route. I know only too well that plans can easily go wrong, but by keeping to certain principles you can minimize your faults. As your standard improves so the way you play the course will alter accordingly, taking on greater challenges, but knowing what is within your limitations is perhaps one of the great keys to scoring consistently well.

THE ABSOLUTE BEGINNER

Once you have learnt to hit the ball in a practice environment, taking that skill onto the course is the next hurdle, which can sometimes prove quite daunting. Always try to play with someone experienced if you can, though not necessarily of a high standard, because they will help you with the etiquette, and make sure that you do not hold others up.

Use the clubs that you are familiar with, even if this means playing just a 7-iron for most long shots. I would encourage you to give yourself a good lie, even sitting the ball on a low tee peg, so that you make life easy, and can enjoy the experience of being on a course. Naturally you cannot do this if you are marking a card, but in social rounds it will only help to encourage you.

If you are taking a lot of shots, play perhaps five or six shots along the fairway, then pick the ball up and go to the green and putt. I know this is not how we really play golf, but for most people there has to be a transition between practice and on-course performance, and getting round the course in a reasonable time can be quite difficult. There is much to learn, and the more you play, the easier it will all become.

THE HIGH HANDICAPPER

Once over that initial on-course learning stage, your sights will be set on playing to a certain standard as often as possible, and this is when you have to think more about your shots. You will begin to know how far you can hit your tee shot and therefore what hazards are within range. If it is possible that you may drive into a hazard, be it water or sand, then check your aim very carefully, or consider using another club so that you cannot reach the hazard. Reread the section on the tee shot in Chapter 5, and be careful where you want the ball to go; do not fall into the trap of slavishly following the line of the tees, which often aim towards the trouble you wish to avoid.

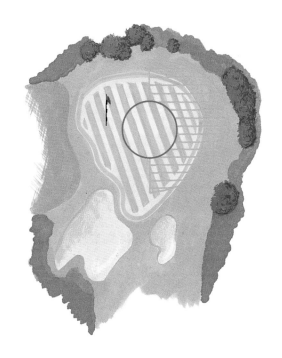

Above: Aim for the centre of the green rather than always going straight for the pin.

Left: Check your aim carefully to make sure you are not aiming at a hazard.

Many ladies have problems with the longer irons and fairway woods, so until such time as you can use them reliably, stick to the medium irons if you feel more comfortable. Do not feel pressurized into using the longer ones simply because your friend might, or because you know that is what you are supposed to do. In golf it is

'how many', not 'how' that is the bottom line.

Aim for the centre of the green, rather than the pin and you will give yourself the best chance of a putt being your next shot.

Play shots that you know are within your capabilities. For instance, if around the green, the ball is not sitting up well and there is a bunker between you and the pin, consider playing a shot not directly aimed at the pin to avoid playing over the bunker. I know that so many shots are lost by the higher handicap players once they hit the ball into a bunker, and from the difficult example that I have given, even a player with a fairly low handicap might struggle.

Whilst the high handicap player is still at the stage of not being very certain of the exact direction the ball may fly, you must start to pay attention to correct aiming, and correct thinking. Earlier in this book I dealt with correct aim and alignment so do get used to having a pre-shot routine. It does not take you any great length of time, and will help to ensure that the good shots do go in the right direction.

You might assume that correct thinking is a waste of time if you are not capable of fulfilling those ideals, but that is nonsense. At this stage you must try to plan your route so that you are less likely to waste shots, mainly by hitting the ball into trouble.

Try to aim away from fairway bunkers, and make the middle of the green your target, rather than always aiming directly at the pin. Remember the Stroke Index system in golf is designed to let you to take your handicap allowance at the hardest holes on the course.

Therefore your personal par at each hole is the par of the card plus your handicap allowance; so for instance, if the hole is a par-4, and you get two shots on it, your par is 6, which means you should aim to get on the green in four shots, plus two shots allowed for putting. This way of approaching the game generally takes a lot of pressure off a player, and makes her goals more attainable.

Plan your way round the course carefully, even if it means aiming away from the hole in order to safely avoid any hazards.

THE MIDDLE AND LOW HANDICAPPER

I would consider this category to include any players of 18 handicap and better, which means that you will have certainly reached the point where planning your round becomes more important, since wasting shots is less tolerable.

Whilst there is a considerable difference in ability between the single figure player and an 18 handicapper, the planning and thinking should be very similar.

As I have already mentioned for the high handicap player, avoiding hazards is important, and this aspect of planning still holds true for the better players. In reality, the further you can hit the ball, more hazards tend to be in range, so from the tee you must consider carefully your options.

Do **not** simply take a driver on all long holes, but play sensibly and use the 3-wood for extra accuracy. Naturally much will depend on the course you play and whether you warm up before a round, but the few yards you might sacrifice by using the 3-wood will be offset by a greater assurance that you will find the fairway.

Try to assess whether one side of the fairway is strategically better; this will be based on where the hazards are placed, and where the pin is situated. If for instance, the hole is on the right hand side of the green, approaching from the left of the fairway will probably be better.

However, if there is a hazard down the left half in range from the tee, then you must weigh up whether the risk of going in it is worth the chance of an easier second shot.

Very often it may require one of your best shots to carry a hazard, in which case, depending on your form that day, it may be better to lay up short with an iron. This does need quite a high degree of self discipline, since most of us would quite happily go for broke far too often.

Try to hit your drive so that you can approach the green from the 'easy' side.

So before playing what you might rate as a slightly risky shot, please give the following some careful consideration.

1. How well are you playing at the time?

All golfers' standards vary from round to round. If it is a good day, then certain shots will seem quite within your capabilities, whereas on one of those days where the swing seems totally mistimed, caution should be the watchword.

Do not let the pin be a magnet. Consider whether aiming at the flag is worth the risk if it means a slightly wayward shot would find sand or water.

2. How is the ball lying?

If the ball is lying badly do not attempt the impossible; settle for keeping it in play, even if it means dropping a shot. By taking a chance you may drop two or more.

3. Is it worth the gamble if it fails?

Each situation will be different, but you need to avoid wasting shots either by having to take penalty drops, or by getting in fairway bunkers unnecessarily. For instance, imagine the ball is in the rough and there is a bunker twenty yards ahead on your line, you need distance, so you select a 5-wood.

Depending on the lie in the rough, there is a danger that the ball could come out low, in which case it could land in the bunker. I am not saying don't take a 5-wood, I am saying **think** of all the possibilities before taking that club.

In the rough think carefully about your options rather than just hitting the first club that comes to hand.

4. Does the situation warrant the risk?

Match play and stroke play will determine your thought processes in this matter. Match play often requires that greater risks are taken: for instance at a short par-5 there is a chance that if you can carry the corner of a dog-leg, you can reach the green in two shots. There is out of bounds at the elbow of the dog-leg, and a bunker fifty yards short of the green. Obviously taking on the challenge is a high risk option,

and not one to take if you are comfortably ahead in your match.

If you are perhaps two down with three to play and feel that your best way to win the hole is to take the chance, then the gamble may be worthwhile.

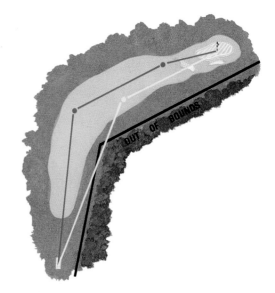

Only take the riskier option if it is really necessary and you feel confident.

If you were playing the same hole in stroke play, and had a good score to that point, then to attempt the carry would be foolish; it would be far wiser to rely on a good third shot to give you the chance of a birdie or a safe par without the risk of penalty shots.

As a lower handicap player you will inevitably have a reasonably good short game, and a greater variety of shots at your disposal.

Always set your goals high enough and remember that generally you are trying to hole shots from around the green; the only time when this thought might not be in your mind is if going past the pin is going to leave you with a very difficult putt.

If you are quite capable of playing a delicate shot over a bunker to a pin cut close to your side of the green, then play it, but don't fall into the trap (sorry about the pun) of trying to be too clever and consequently hitting it into the bunker. Even the scratch player is better having a ten foot putt to save par rather than having to hole a bunker shot.

If you are happy playing over a bunker then do so; though you might have to work hard if the pin is cut close to your side of the green.

Be positive with your putting, but not to the extent that you might turn an easy two-putt situation into a three-putt nightmare. Always visualize the ball falling into the hole at a speed that would take it only about one or two feet past the hole should it miss.

I am absolutely convinced that not enough thought goes into most club golfers' rounds, and I hope that by reading this chapter this aspect of your game will improve, but I would recommend the really keen golfer to have a

playing lesson with their professional, who will be able to talk them through the way to approach the more difficult situations, and show them how to avoid wasting shots.

CLUB SELECTION

The absolute beginner should adhere to the advice offered in the earlier part of this chapter, but all other golfers should consider the following before selecting their club:

1. Is the lie good enough for the club selected?
2. Will the wind affect the ball's flight in some way?
3. Is there trouble short of or past the green?
4. Is the shot uphill or downhill?
5. Is the pin at the front, middle or back of the green?

Use any yardage charts there are to help take the guesswork out of club selection.

Do try to think carefully before simply pulling out the same club for the same shot each round. More players finish short of a green than ever hit past the flag, but by taking one club more you may save yourself several shots during the round.

As you become more consistent do take the time to discover how far you do hit each club. On a calm day hit 15 to 20 shots with your 5-iron, then pace the distance to the centre of the group, ignoring those that are very short and those that are very long. This will give you your average distance for that iron.

By repeating the process with the other clubs (or perhaps alternate clubs, adding or subtracting about ten yards per club) you will know your distance with each club in the bag.

Make use of any available yardage charts and pace any appropriate distances, making note of them if you are playing your regular course.

This takes all the guesswork out of club selection.

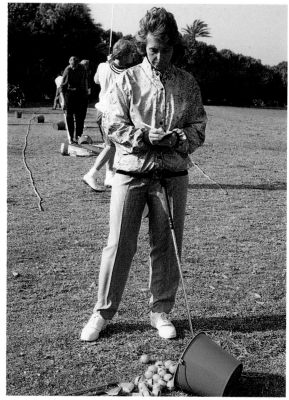

Above: Make a note, on the practice range, of how far you hit the ball with each club.

Left: You will then know which club to use when out on the course, whatever the distance and conditions.

CONCENTRATION

To play golf well requires concentration, but it is not constant throughout the round of golf as you need to be able to switch it on and off at will, as well as the ability to block out all extraneous thoughts for about thirty seconds to two minutes at a time. If you try to concentrate for the entire round you will be exhausted, and your golf will not improve.

Whether you chat between shots with your partner will depend very much on the importance of the round and probably your playing partner. Ideally you must relax between shots.

Deep breathing may help to this end in a tense situation. Under pressure most of us quicken our movements, so try to keep the pace of your game under check, especially if you are playing very well or very badly, as these are the two extremes that tend to cause us to panic.

Do not waste valuable concentration thinking either of shots that you have already played in the round, or those yet to be played. Think only of the shot in hand, and give that your one hundred per cent attention. When you have reached your ball, visualize the shot, select your club, have a practice swing if necessary, then play the shot.

Try to keep to your pre-shot routine; next time you watch professionals play golf, notice that prior to each shot their routine remains constant, which helps them to place equal importance on each shot regardless of the real situation.

We all vary on how much attention we must pay to our actual swing during the round. Many professionals will concentrate solely on rhythm if their swing is sound, while others like to have a key thought, which may change regularly.

Only by experience will you find the best way to attain your true potential, but do not get bogged down in too many swing thoughts on the course; save that for the practice ground. Personally I found one of the most successful ways to play well was to think of the clubhead's path through impact, which allowed me to swing in a very free manner. Any mechanical changes necessary to permit the correct swing path were made in practice.

Take a few moments to concentrate on every shot, even when practising.

EQUIPMENT

When I first started playing golf in 1965, the choice of clubs was very limited. There were basically only four types of shaft flex, and the simple blade head. Nowadays there is the most amazing choice of flexed and coloured shafts, flex points, swing weights and grip sizes, which to the uninformed can seem quite bewildering. Let me try to clarify a few points for you and to give you some sensible guidelines when buying clubs.

GRIP

Generally speaking, the best grip thickness for you is one that allows the fingers of your left hand to almost touch the base of the thumb. A grip too thick will tend to restrict good hand action; one too thin will enliven hand action but you may not have a firm enough hold on the club.

If you change the grips on your clubs, a thinner grip will have the effect of making the club feel heavier when swung, whilst a thicker grip will make it feel lighter.

SHAFT

Ladies shafts are generally called 'L' shafts, although many manufacturers now use various numbers to grade shaft flexes. For most ladies the 'L' shaft is the correct one, since its extra flexibility will promote distance.

The stronger players will need a firmer shaft, sometimes referred to as an 'A' shaft – which is between a ladies' (L) and men's regular (R) shaft. Not all manufacturers produce this shaft under this name, but will probably have an equivalent in their range.

The very strong or the exceptionally tall woman can use a man's regular or 'R' shaft, which is longer and firmer than the 'L' and 'A'. These are used in most men's sets, but do vary in their exact stiffness of flex from one make to another.

Graphite shafts are very good for ladies' clubs since their lightness and construction tend to promote distance. The only problem I find is that there are so many to choose from, and some suit one player and not another. Before you go to the additional expense of graphite shafts, do hit some shots with them, or make use of a trial club if your professional has one.

The difference between a blade (lower) and cavity backed club (upper) is clearly visible in this photograph.

CLUBHEAD

Without doubt, club golfers should use a peripherally-weighted head, where the back of the head is hollowed out, with most of the weight around the edges. This configuration enlarges the sweet spot (the optimum point of contact), and therefore makes the clubs more forgiving of off-centre strikes. The Ping clubs which I use and have featured throughout this book, are in this category.

The other type of head is the blade, which has a flatter back with the weight distributed more evenly throughout the head. Whilst some low handicap players may prefer this type of head, the average golfer would be well advised to avoid it.

SWING WEIGHT

This refers to the method of measuring how heavy the club feels when swung, ranging from about C0 at the lighter end, up to D2 and beyond at the heavy end.

Most ladies' clubs vary between C3 to C8, which is quite a difference. The beginner and average club lady golfer who may not be very strong should go for ladies' clubs at the lighter end, which will include most of those readily available from professionals' shops.

The stronger club golfer, or someone who may be new to golf but quite athletic, may need heavier ladies' clubs or those in the lighter end of the men's range.

Avoid any clubs that feel heavy to swing, as you must have control of them even at the end of the round when you may feel tired.

THE LIE

This refers mainly to irons, and is the angle at which the base of the iron sits when you address the ball.

With the correct lie the toe end of the club should be just off the ground.

If the club is too upright the toe sits too much up in the air and the heel can tend to catch on the turf at impact, possibly causing pulled or hooked shots.

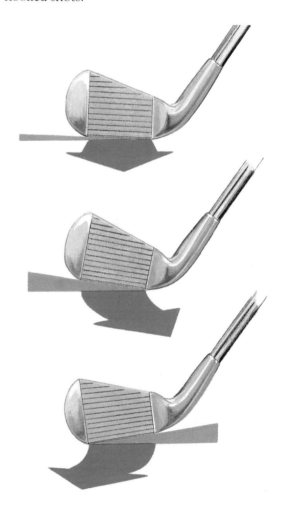

If the lie of an iron is correct (top) the toe sits just off the ground. With an upright lie (centre) the toe sits off the ground too much and causes hooked shots. With a flat lie (bottom) the heel sits off the ground and causes sliced shots.

If the club is too flat, the heel sits off the ground, and the toe can tend to catch on the turf at impact causing pushed or faded shots.

Most, although not all, clubs can have the lie adjusted, so check this aspect with the professional before you buy them.

WOODS

The greatest innovation in recent years has been metal woods which have a similar construction to the peripherally weighted iron, thus making them very forgiving of bad shots. It is not essential to have matching woods and irons, although clubs of similar swing weight are an advantage. Most club golfers do not need a driver; opt instead for a 3-wood and 5-wood, then buy a driver when your ability improves. You might also consider including a 7-wood in the bag, which would certainly be of more benefit than the driver for most players.

The metal wood has been one of the most significant advances in club design of recent years.

A selection of woods – the choice these days is amazing, so take your time and find the clubs that suit you.

PUTTERS

The easiest putters to use are those with heel and toe weighting, which enlarges the sweet spot and makes them more tolerant of off-centre strikes. The putter head should sit reasonably flat on the ground, and this will be affected very much by the length of the putter shaft.

Standing at five feet, three inches, I usually need my putter shafts shortened so that they do not catch on my jumper. Your professional can easily tailor yours so that the putter head sits as recommended.

Putters come in various styles. Choose one that you feel comfortable with.

TRY BEFORE YOU BUY

This advice must be the watchword. I think it is important that you like the look of your clubs, but most importantly you must feel comfortable hitting the ball with them. Ideally you should select several clubs to try so that you get a comparison of feel, distance and accuracy.

Do not assume that the most expensive, usually a graphite shafted set, will be the best for you. Do not rush into buying a new set, try friends' clubs if possible; take time to find the correct clubs for you.

GOLF BALLS

These basically fall into three categories:

1. Wound Balata covered

This ball has a small inner core covered by wound elastic, which is covered in Balata. This soft material spins quickly when hit, which has the effect of emphasising a fade or draw, or backspin. The professionals use this ball as they almost unerringly apply the spin they intend.

For the club golfer this can be a disastrous ball to use, as unwanted sidespin causes the ball to veer even further off-line than usual. The ball also cuts and scuffs more readily, so only the low handicap golfers would really benefit from the extra control that this ball gives.

2. Wound Surlyn covered

This ball is constructed the same as the one above except that the cover is harder, and therefore does not spin as fast nor mark so readily. This is probably the best ball for many golfers, especially if length is not your problem, or if the course is running fast. It is more controllable than the solid golf ball, but does not generally go as far.

3. Solid Surlyn covered

This ball has a solid rather than a wound core and is covered in Surlyn. These factors promote length, although a certain amount of control, especially around the green, is lost compared to a wound ball. For the average golfer this ball would be the best choice, as it does not mark easily, and its additional length is worth having at the expense of some control.

CARE OF YOUR EQUIPMENT

Your clubs are expensive items and need careful care and attention. You should regularly scrub the grips to keep them free of grease, and check that the grooves are not filled with dirt. If your woods are wooden, be sure to use head covers, and get any loose whipping repaired immediately.

If you have graphite shafts extra care should be taken and it is wise to have a golf bag with soft dividers so that the shafts do not get worn.

You should also regularly check your shoes, replacing any worn or loose studs.

The low handicap player may find it useful to have the lofts and lies of her clubs checked each year, since these can alter slightly, particularly if you practise at a driving range.

If your clubs get wet, remove them from the bag as soon as possible, wipe them down and let them dry at room temperature, removing the head covers from the woods.

Your shoes are vitally important to you yet so many golfers take less care of these heavy duty shoes than they do their normal daytime footwear. You can buy two types, those with spikes and those with moulded soles, which are better for the summer. If you have spikes make sure you replace them once they become worn.

EXERCISES

Whilst your strength will improve the more you play, it is also a good idea to do some exercises, especially in the winter when, with the weather being as it often is, you might play less golf. Don't, however, get the idea that I am going to suggest you spend hours in an aerobics class or the gym 'pumping iron' as the men say.

Remember that in golf it is suppleness that counts as well as strength, and the older we get so both tend to wane. However, if you retain your suppleness you will at least be able to make a good turn, which is crucial for you if you are to hit the ball the maximum distance for you.

Fortunately, in golf, it is not supreme physical fitness that makes you a good golfer, but physical fitness does enhance mental fitness, so do not neglect this aspect.

To improve your hand and arm strength, hit a medium iron (5-iron) through rough grass. For this exercise find a part of the practice area where the grass is longer, rather than on the course itself.

Stand with your feet apart, your knees flexed and your arms horizontal. Swing your arms and turn your body to the right and left, gently stretching the back muscles. The further you turn the more you will feel a stretching sensation in your back, but be careful not to strain anything. Stretch slowly and gradually extend yourself.

Keep each heel on the ground if you can, but if not let them rise very slightly at the limit of each turn. This is also a very good exercise to do before you play.

To increase your forearm and hand power, practise wringing out a towel, although it need not be wet. This can even be done indoors sitting in an armchair. Squeezing a squash ball will have a similar effect.

Swing two clubs together. Although you will find it difficult to hold them perfectly together, and will never be able to adopt the correct grip, this is a great exercise for building a good, smooth rhythm, as well as for stretching your muscles. Again this is a wonderful warm-up exercise before you go out on the course.

Cycling, for real in the open air or on an exercise bicycle at home, will improve your leg strength. If you cannot cycle, skipping or doing leg squats will increase your ability to play a round of golf without feeling too tired.

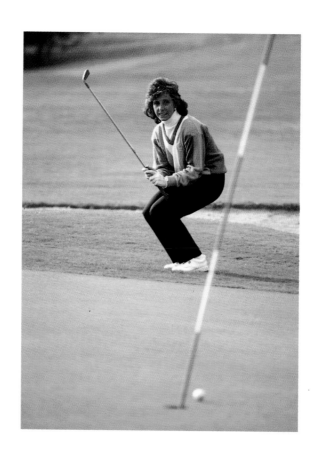

Whatever targets you set for yourself, always
remember to enjoy this wonderful game of golf.

This book belongs in the Home Library of:

© Nick Butterworth
www.myhomelibrary.org

This book belongs in the home library of . . . .

© Mick Inkpen
www.myhomelibrary.org

STORIES RETOLD BY –
ELAINE IFE
ROSALIND SUTTON
ILLUSTRATED BY –
ERIC ROWE
RUSSELL LEE
GEORGE FRYER